HOW SCIENCE WORKS

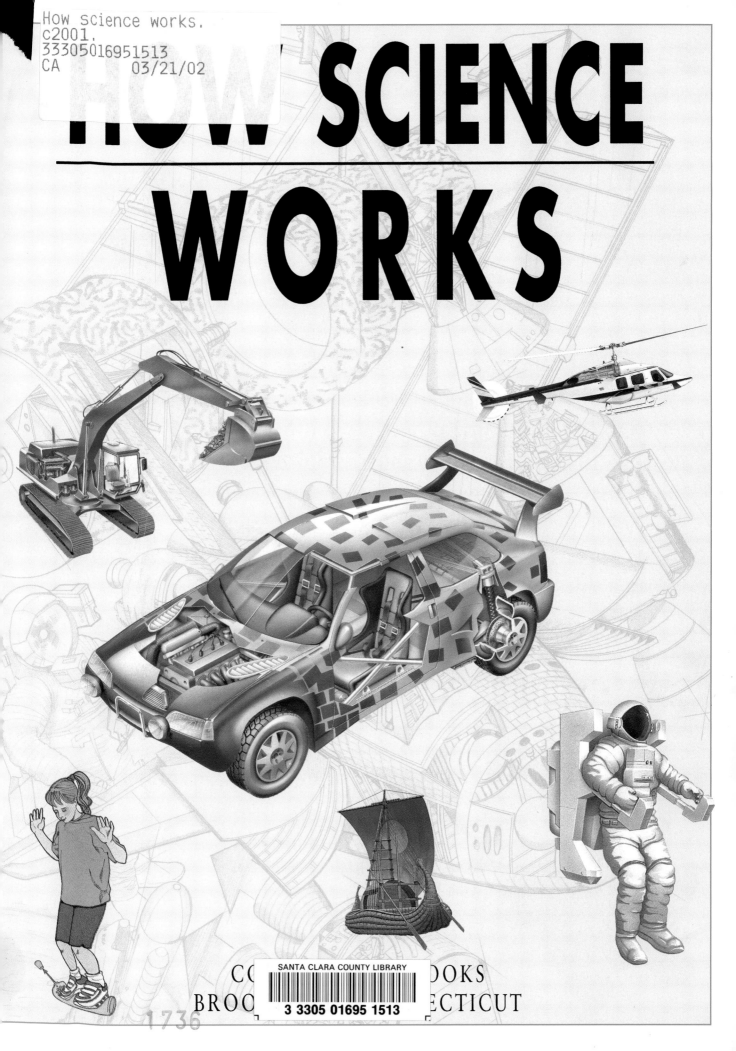

CO   OOKS
BROO   ECTICUT

1736

INTRODUCTION

There are many different types of vehicle that humans use. Some of them help us move about from place to place, others are machines that help us do a particular job. All of them are designed and built so they can move in certain ways, move at certain speeds, or perform certain tasks. You can read all about the science behind many kinds of vehicle.

In the first chapter, we look at *rockets* and *spacecraft*. The rockets that launch spacecraft into space are huge and powerful. Yet they work in much the same way as fireworks. Both get their power by burning fuel. As they burn, hot gases push out of the back of the rocket, driving the rocket forward. See how you can build a rocket that soars high into the sky.

In chapter two, discover the science that makes *cars*, *trains*, and *motorcycles* work. All land vehicles have wheels, and they all need engines to drive them forward. They also all need brakes to stop. Test your knowledge by building a model car.

In chapter three, you can look inside *ships* and *submarines* to understand the basic science of seacraft. From a tiny rowboat to a cruise liner carrying hundreds of passengers, they all have to stay afloat. If you follow the projects you can build a model ship.

Read about the many different types of *aircraft* in chapter four. Most planes use the flow of air over their wings to provide lift, and propellers or jets to drive them forward. But all planes fly in much the same way. Then you can build a fantastic glider that really flies!

Finally, chapter five looks at how *trucks*, *tractors*, and *cranes* lift and move heavy loads. Modern tractors and cranes use complex hydraulic and electronic systems. Find out how to build your own model crane or digger that can actually pick things up.

© Aladdin Books Ltd 2001

Designed and produced by
Aladdin Books Ltd
28 Percy Street
London W1P 0LD

First published in
the United States in 2001 by
Copper Beech Books,
an imprint of
The Millbrook Press
2 Old New Milford Road
Brookfield, Connecticut 06804

ISBN 0-7613-2278-7 (Trade Pbk.)

*Cataloging-in-Publication Data is
on file at the Library of Congress*
Printed in UAE
Editors
Jim Pipe
Mark Jackson

Science Consultant
Bryson Gore

Series Design
David West Children's Books

Designer
Simon Morse

Illustrators
Simon Bishop, Peter Harper,
Ron Hayward, Aziz Khan, Alex
Pang, Francis Phillipps,
Richard Rockwood,
David Russell, Rob Shone,
Don Simpson—Specs Art,
Simon Tegg, Ian Thompson,
Catherine Ward, Ross Watton,
Graham White, Gerald Witcomb

Picture Research
Brooks Krikler Research

CONTENTS

CHAPTER 4—AIRCRAFT

CHAPTER 5—TRUCKS, TRACTORS, CRANES

CHAPTER 1—SPACECRAFT
THE SCIENCE OF SPACE

Huge teams of scientists are needed to develop the technology to send spacecraft into space. They have to build powerful rockets to lift the spacecraft above the Earth and into an orbit.

Once in space, some spacecraft are controlled by automation from the ground. Others have a crew, and the spacecraft must be built to carry them safely.

Rocket fuels burn so fiercely that rockets must be built from special materials.

Nose cone

Satellite

Outer shell

CONTROLS

There are no wheels to steer with in space. Instead, spacecraft are guided by small "booster" rockets on the side. These are turned to push the spacecraft in the right direction.

Mir space station

Space shuttle

LIVING IN SPACE

Once in space, the crew are out on their own. The spacecraft must provide all their needs and protect them from dangerous radiation. Inside the spacecraft the crew and everything else appear weightless. This makes even showering tricky!

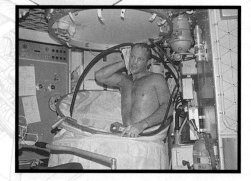

WHAT IS SPACE?

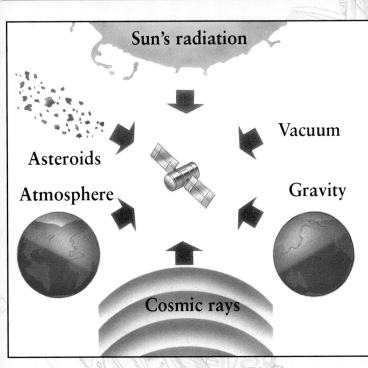

Sun's radiation

Vacuum

Asteroids

Atmosphere

Gravity

Cosmic rays

Rocket scientists have to think about what space is like. Gravity and Earth's atmosphere still affect a spacecraft when it is in orbit, but the vacuum that exists in space creates other problems, too.

Harmful rays from the Sun and the rest of the Universe can also damage a spacecraft, as can even tiny pieces of floating rock.

CONSTRUCTION

Venera

Lunar module

Most rockets are quite similar, but the small spacecraft they carry vary enormously. Venera was made to visit Venus. The lunar probe was designed for an unmanned visit to the Moon. The lunar module was designed to land astronauts on the Moon's surface.

Fuel tanks

Lunar probe

To make the projects, you will need: a plastic bottle, paper, cardboard, balsa wood, a craft knife, a drill, scissors, craft glue, strong epoxy glue, a ruler, a pencil, oil-based paints, tinfoil, a cork, and a bicycle pump and valve.

Rocket project box

Science experiment project box

Burner where the fuels burn

INTO SPACE

One of the hardest things for spacecraft to do is to actually get off the ground. To climb into space, a spacecraft needs to overcome gravity, the force of attraction that holds everything on the ground. So far, the only way scientists have found of doing this is to use huge rockets to thrust spacecraft upward against gravity.

Break out! If a rocket is launched with enough power, it can break free of Earth's gravity.

When you hold a tennis ball and a grapefruit (*above*), the different weights that you feel are the force of Earth's gravity pulling on their two different masses.

Mass and weight

Fill a balloon with water and it feels very heavy. Now lower the balloon into water. You will see that it feels much lighter. This is because the pressure of the water outside is lifting it up. Weight is a measure of the pull of gravity, and it can change. This is why scientists talk about "mass." This is the amount of matter in an object. It's the same wherever you measure it.

Airplanes only climb a short way above the ground, where the pull of gravity is still strong.

GRAVITY

Gravity doesn't only hold things on the ground. It is the force of attraction between every bit of matter in the Universe. It is the force that makes Earth and all the other planets stay close to the Sun and continue circling it.

Sun

Moon

The Moon stays in orbit (circling Earth) because the Moon and Earth are pulled together by each other's gravity.

Satellites stay up because they are moving too fast to fall. Their speed balances out the pull of Earth's gravity.

Gravity gets weaker higher up, so a satellite circling Earth low down has to travel much faster to stay up.

LOSING WEIGHT

Astronauts in spacecraft orbiting Earth float around freely as if they were weightless. This is because the spacecraft is whizzing around the planet so fast that a force, called centrifugal force, balances the effect of gravity. Astronauts practice being weightless by flying in a plane that falls so fast that they float off the floor (*top*).

FORCES NEEDED

Airplanes use the pressure of air on their wings to lift them up. But there is no air far above Earth and wings would be useless.

So rocket engines alone must develop enough "thrust," or push, to overcome the spacecraft's weight.

The British scientist Sir Isaac Newton (1642–1727) discovered many of the laws about momentum. Momentum is what keeps a moving object going in a straight line unless a force acts on it.

TYPES OF ENERGY

Energy comes in two forms. Potential energy (PE) is energy stored up ready for action, like the unburned fuel in a rocket.

Kinetic energy (KE) is the energy something has because it is moving, like a rocket traveling through space.

NEWTON'S FIRST LAW

Newton's first law states that to make an object go faster or slower, you need a force. This is because its momentum keeps it going at the same speed and in the same direction. If an astronaut pushed himself away from a spacecraft, he could drift off into space forever, as there is nothing in space to stop him.

A spacecraft coming back to Earth is traveling very fast, but it relies on friction with the air to slow it down. This is why it gets very hot.

TRAVEL IN SPACE

Moving through space is very different from moving on the ground. When a car moves, its wheels push against the ground. As soon as they stop pushing, friction slows the car down. In empty space, there is nothing to stop a spacecraft from moving —but there is nothing to push against either, not even air. So how does a spacecraft move?

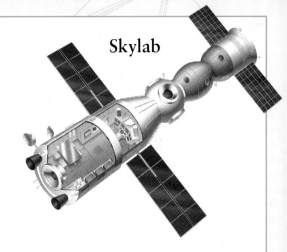
Skylab

Space stations need only a little power to keep them in orbit because they are moving through space very fast, so they have a lot of momentum.

In space, a rocket is kept going by its own momentum and a few bursts from booster rockets.

The secret of space travel

You can't push unless there's something to push against. Newton's third law shows how, when a force pushes one way, an equal force pushes in the opposite direction. If you throw a ball while on roller skates, you will roll back a little in reaction as the ball moves forward. Rockets move through space in the same way.

As the burning fuels expand behind a rocket, they push it forward in an equal and opposite reaction. When an astronaut opens a hatch in space, her body also turns in an opposite reaction.

NEWTON'S SECOND LAW

The amount something speeds up or slows down—the acceleration—depends on just how strong the force is and how heavy the object is. The heavier a rocket is, the more force it needs to get it into space. A big car is also harder to get moving than a small car.

ROCKET POWER

Some rockets, such as booster rockets, burn a solid, rubbery fuel, but most are powered by liquid fuel. Liquid fuel only burns with oxygen, but there is no oxygen far above the ground. So the rocket must also carry a chemical that provides oxygen, called an oxidizer. The fuel and oxidizer mix in a combustion chamber, then a spark called an igniter sets them alight.

Blow up a balloon and let it go. It darts about as it reacts against the air rushing out of it. Rockets work in much the same way.

Ariane V blasts off

LIQUID FUEL ROCKETS

Different rockets use different fuels—the space shuttle uses liquid hydrogen, and Saturn V used kerosene. Most types of fuel are pumped into the combustion chamber with an oxidizer such as liquid oxygen (or LOX). Here, they burn together to create a high pressure stream of gases that roars out through a small nozzle at speeds of about 9,000 mph.

The nozzle is shaped so that the gases roar out of the rocket at the maximum speed and pressure.

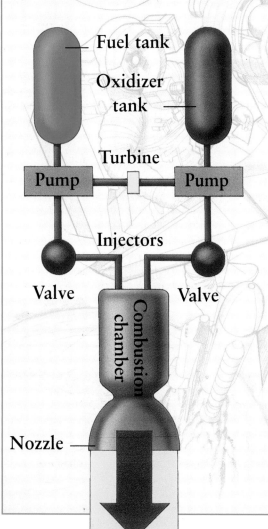

Fuel tank

Oxidizer tank

Turbine

Pump

Pump

Injectors

Valve

Valve

Combustion chamber

Nozzle

Too narrow

Too wide

For the first few minutes of flight, the rocket's speed is limited by gravity and, as it speeds up, friction with the air. As it climbs higher, these get less and less.

As it burns more fuel, the rocket itself gets lighter. Once in space, it needs only a little fuel to keep it going.

Liquid oxygen

Fuel line

Liquid hydrogen

LIQUID FUEL ROCKET

Nozzle

MODEL ROCKET
PART 1
NOZZLE

ADULT HELP NEEDED

1 Find a cork that fits a half-gallon plastic bottle. Then ask an adult to drill a hole through it just wide enough for a valve to fit tightly.

2 Seal the surface of the cork by painting craft glue over the outside of it, but leave the hole free of glue.

3 When the glue is dry, push the valve through the hole in the cork. Use the same sort of valve you would use to pump up a football or basketball.

ARIANE V

Rocket fuel burns incredibly quickly, and most rockets only have enough fuel to last a few minutes. The main engine in the Ariane V rocket (see page 14) burns for ten minutes. In this time it uses 158 tons of fuel.

Ariane V

MMUs

MMU

You don't have to burn rocket fuel to move around in space. Forcing any gas out through a nozzle will provide a push in the opposite direction.

The Manned Maneuvering Units (MMUs) that astronauts strap on their backs for spacewalks use jets of cold nitrogen gas in this way.

Nozzles pointing in different directions (*right*) move the MMU and steer it in the direction the astronaut wants to go.

OTHER ROCKET ENGINES

In rockets powered with liquid fuels, the fuels weigh an enormous amount and are dangerously explosive. So space engineers have experimented with other engines.

Solid-fuel rockets are already used. But scientists are trying other ideas, including NERVA engines (*below*). These pump hydrogen gas at high pressure into a nuclear reactor. This creates a powerful jet that propels the rocket into space.

Booster

NERVA ENGINE

Bottles pump in hydrogen

Liquid oxygen

Once ignited, solid-fuel engines usually cannot be stopped or restarted, so they are generally used for short missions or for small booster rockets that make fine changes to direction.

Liquid hydrogen

Solid fuel

SOLID-FUEL ROCKETS

Parachutes allow boosters to fall back to Earth.

Solid-fuel rocket engines are the oldest of all engines. They were used by the Chinese almost a thousand years ago. They are basically rods of solid fuel with a tube down the middle. When the fuel is ignited, it burns out through the tube. In the space shuttle, the fuel lasts about two minutes.

Nuclear reactor

Nozzle

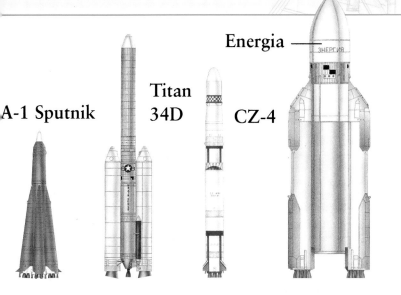

A-1 Sputnik

Titan 34D

Energia

CZ-4

THE NEW SHUTTLE

If the Venture Star (*below*) is a success, flights into space could be as routine as flights on an airplane. With its "linear airspike" engines—rockets arranged in rows—Venture Star can take off and land again and again like an airplane.

SPACE SHUTTLE

Rocket launchers have grown bigger and bigger over the last 50 years (*above*).

Cargo bay

Main engine

Wings for gliding

DANGER: EXPLOSIVE!

Scientists do all they can to reduce accidents, but space travel is risky. When a spacecraft takes off on liquid-fuel rockets, it is riding on a giant bomb. In 1986, the space shuttle Challenger (*below*) blew up on liftoff.

The space shuttle is one of the few spacecraft that uses solid-fuel rockets to boost it into space. The shuttle has two solid-rocket boosters (SRBs) as well as three main engines, each powered by liquid fuel from a big strap-on tank.

Third stage

Nose cone falls away

Satellite

Most satellites need to be protected to cope with the force of gravity during liftoff. Some are launched inside the nose cone of the rocket, which falls away just like the booster sections (*left*).

CONSTRUCTION

Second stage

To cope with the kind of energy needed to thrust a spacecraft high into the sky, rockets have to be incredibly tough. Temperatures in the combustion chamber of a solid-fuel rocket can soar well over 5000° F. Yet rockets have to be light, too. So engineers build them from tough, light materials such as titanium.

Boosters

First stage

MODEL ROCKET
PART 2
THE BODY & FINS

1 Use the plan on page 26 to mark out a fin onto balsa wood. Then get an adult to help you cut out four identical fins using a craft knife.

2 Glue the fins to the bottom of a half-gallon plastic bottle with strong epoxy glue, so that they form a cross pattern (*right*).

BOOSTER STAGES

The amount of fuel needed to launch most spacecraft is still so huge that most rockets are simply giant fuel tanks. Once a spacecraft has escaped the pull of Earth's gravity, there is no need for all this fuel. So the rockets are built in stages that fall away as the spacecraft climbs higher and fuel is burned up.

LIGHT BUT STRONG

Rockets are built like giant tin cans. It's easy to squeeze a soda can in at the sides. But you'll find it's almost impossible to squeeze it from the ends. This is because the rigid rim of the can spreads the pressure of your squeeze through the length of the can. Rockets are light and strong in the same way.

Space stations that are far too big to launch are put together in space, section by section, by astronauts (*above*).

The sides of some rockets are not thick metal sheets, but two thin sheets separated by a honeycomb of very thin metal boxes (*right*). This structure is light and strong.

First stage

Second stage

Third stage

SATURN V
ROCKET

Lunar modules

Lunar modules

Third stage

Second stage

First stage

SHAPES IN SPACE

On Earth, friction between the air and a vehicle's surface causes drag. This force slows a vehicle down. Out in space, there is no air, and it doesn't really matter what shape a spacecraft is. Probes (*right*) are often awkward shapes, with parts sticking out at all angles.

The Viking probe (*belo...* was sent to look for li... on Mar...

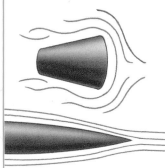

Spacecraft coming back to Earth have a flat front, so that the air acts as a brake.

Rockets have a pointed nose to slice through the air.

DRAG

Drag is a force that slows moving objects down when a gas or liquid flows past them. You can feel the effect of drag by pulling your hand through a bowl of water.

Viking lander

Solar panels

Solar panels catch the Sun's rays and provide probes with energy.

Fuel tanks

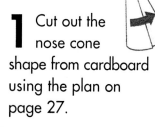

MODEL ROCKET

PART 3

THE NOSE

3 Then glue the nose cone to the base of the plastic bottle—the top of the rocket.

1 Cut out the nose cone shape from cardboard using the plan on page 27.

2 To make the cone, overlap the two straight sides of the nose cone shape and glue them together.

THE PAYLOAD

When a spacecraft takes off, most of its weight is fuel and fuel tanks. The space shuttle weighs only 75 tons, but the total weight of the fuel tanks, rockets, and fuel needed to blast it into space is 2,000 tons. The amount the shuttle can carry in its cargo bay is just 30 tons.

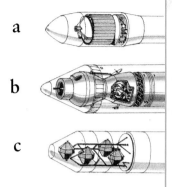

a

b

c

The payload is what rockets carry into space, such as (*above*):
a) probe—a spacecraft with no crew
b) mission with human crew
c) satellites

REENTRY

When the wind blows very hard, it can make your face sting. But imagine the force when a shuttle traveling at over 12,000 mph reenters Earth's atmosphere. The friction with the air makes the shuttle very hot. So its nose and underside are coated with heat-resistant ceramic tiles.

During their descent, spacecraft are pulled by gravity like any other object. In some cases, small space capsules use parachutes to slow the last bit of their fall (*right*).

Shuttles fly back to Earth under their own power—like an airplane.

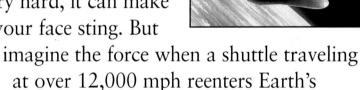

Too shallow

Correct angle

Too deep

A shuttle must reenter at the correct angle. If it comes in too shallow, it bounces off the atmosphere; if it aims too deep, it burns up.

WHAT IS SPACE?

As you go higher and higher, Earth's atmosphere gets thinner and thinner. Eventually, about 550 miles up, it fades away into space.

Space is the vast, black emptiness between planets and stars. In space, there is not even air to breathe. But it is constantly crossed by streams of dangerous radiation from the Sun and other stars.

WHERE IT STARTS

It is hard to say where the atmosphere ends and space begins. For astronauts, space starts at an altitude of 80 miles, the lowest height a spacecraft can stay in orbit. On the ground you can drive that distance in an hour—so space is not far from the surface of our planet.

The atmosphere only fades off into empty space in a layer called the exosphere. The exosphere starts at 480 miles above ground.

Gasp!

A portion of air is oxygen, the gas most things, such as rocket fuel, need to burn. But there is no oxygen (or any other gas) in space. To see what happens when oxygen is used up, get an adult to try this experiment.

1 Stand a candle in a shallow bowl of water. The water makes sure no extra air can reach the candle.

2 Light the candle. Place a glass jar over it. After a while, the candle goes out. This is because most of the oxygen in the jar has been used up.

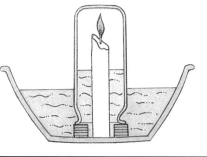

Thermosphere (50-480 miles up) Temp. from -248°F to 3632°F.

Jet

Surface

Sea level—The temperature on the surface is about 52°F.

MODEL ROCKET
PART 4
PROTECTION

1 Use acrylic paint to paint the rocket's nose and tail fins. Wrap tinfoil around the body of the rocket, with the shiny side facing outward.

2 Try this experiment to see how spacecraft can be protected in space. Fill two bottles with water. Wrap one in tinfoil and paint the other black. Leave them in the sunshine. After an hour, feel each bottle. The bottle wrapped in foil will feel much cooler than the black one, because the Sun's rays bounce off the shiny foil.

Spacesuits stop astronauts from getting too hot or cold. They also shield against the Sun's rays. We are normally protected from these rays by Earth's atmosphere (but we can get sunburned).

Shuttle

Stratosphere (8-34 miles up)
Temp. from -106° to 50°F.

EARTH

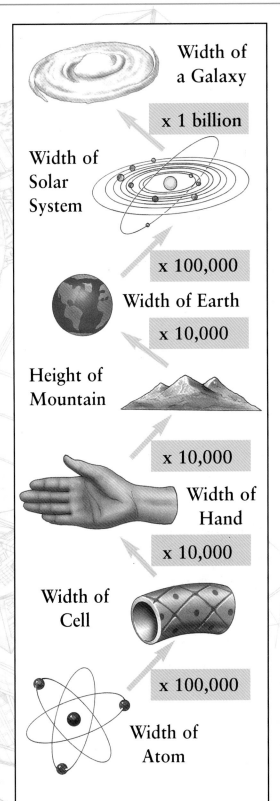

Width of a Galaxy

x 1 billion

Width of Solar System

x 100,000

Width of Earth

x 10,000

Height of Mountain

x 10,000

Width of Hand

x 10,000

Width of Cell

x 100,000

Width of Atom

Astronomers only began to realize how big space is about 70 years ago. The chart above shows you just how big space is, compared to things around us.

LIVING IN SPACE

When astronauts travel into space, the spacecraft must not only protect them from radiation in space, it must also provide all they need in order to breathe, eat, drink, and sleep. Once in orbit, the astronauts have to deal with weightlessness. This means that things float freely because gravity does not hold them down (see page 9).

To run the equipment onboard, a spacecraft needs a lot of energy. In addition to solar panels (*above*), spacecraft have batteries to store electricity to use when they are in Earth's shadow.

Port to link up with other spacecraft

Escape capsule

Laboratories

SPACE FOOD

Space food must be healthy and easy to use and store. On early missions, astronauts ate dried and powdered food to which they added water. Now they have prepared meals, like microwave meals at home (*above*).

When the International Space Station (*below*) is finished, it will be 355 feet long and 295 feet wide.

It will provide a complete environment for dozens of people to work in space for months at a time.

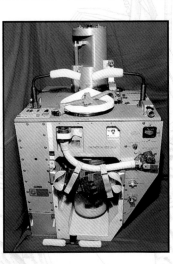

KEEPING A BALANCE

To survive, astronauts need oxygen as well as food and drink (*below*). Machines in spacecraft provide oxygen and remove the carbon dioxide that the astronauts breathe out. Space toilets (*left*) save the water from bodily waste and blast the dry matter into space.

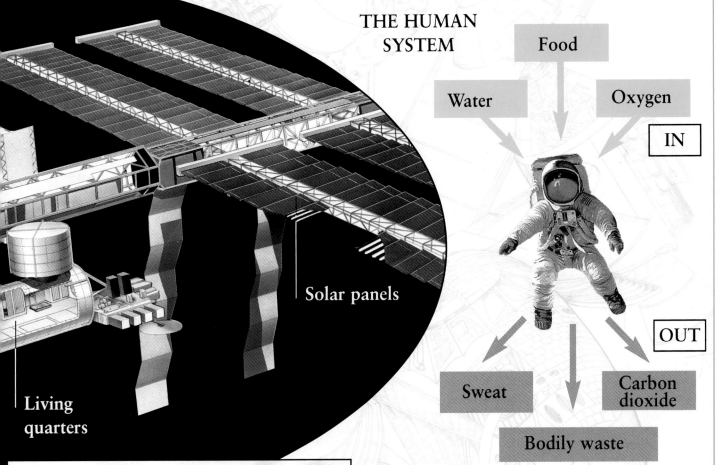

THE HUMAN SYSTEM

Food

Water

Oxygen

IN

Solar panels

OUT

Living quarters

Sweat

Bodily waste

Carbon dioxide

BIODOMES

Only Earth allows humans to live without any protection. If we are ever to live on other planets, it will have to be inside completely sealed buildings (like the Biosphere 2 experiment, *left*) that provide all our needs, just like a spacecraft.

COMMUNICATIONS

The launch

Even far out in space, astronauts and spacecraft can keep in touch with mission control on the ground in a number of ways. Astronauts talk to mission control by radio. Television pictures are beamed back to Earth. Computers, sensors, and other equipment on the spacecraft send back streams of signals via radio waves.

This shuttle cockpit (*above*) shows the huge number of control systems that are needed in a spacecraft.

Sometimes signals can be beamed directly between the space shuttle and mission control.

Shuttle

Relay satellite

MISSION CONTROL

Mission control (*above*) follows every spacecraft constantly, but the link is not always easy to maintain. Sometimes the spacecraft may move out of sight on the other side of the world, or on the far side of a planet. Important messages are often printed out so they can be checked.

When the shuttle is out of sight, signals sometimes have to be bounced off a relay satellite.

Fuel tanks
released

Maneuver
for reentry

Launch satellite

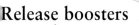

Release boosters

MODEL ROCKET
PART 5
BLAST OFF!

Reentry

1 Pour about two cups of water into your rocket. Put a bicycle valve inside a cork and place the cork firmly into the neck of the bottle. Attach a bicycle pump to the valve and stand the rocket on its fins on a hard surface outside. Pump air into your rocket until it blasts off.

WARNING: DO NOT STAND OVER THE ROCKET AS THE AIR IS PUMPED IN.

2 Find out what level of water gives the best results.

Glides back
to Earth

Blast off

SHUTTLE MISSION

The space shuttle was the first reusable spacecraft. It is often used for carrying satellites into space or repairing them in orbit. It is also used to ferry crew members to and from space stations.

If your car breaks down, you can take it to be repaired. In space, it's not quite so easy! When the Mir space station got damaged (*left*), it cost millions of dollars to keep it in orbit. In the end, the station will be abandoned.

PLANS FOR MODEL ROCKET

Fin

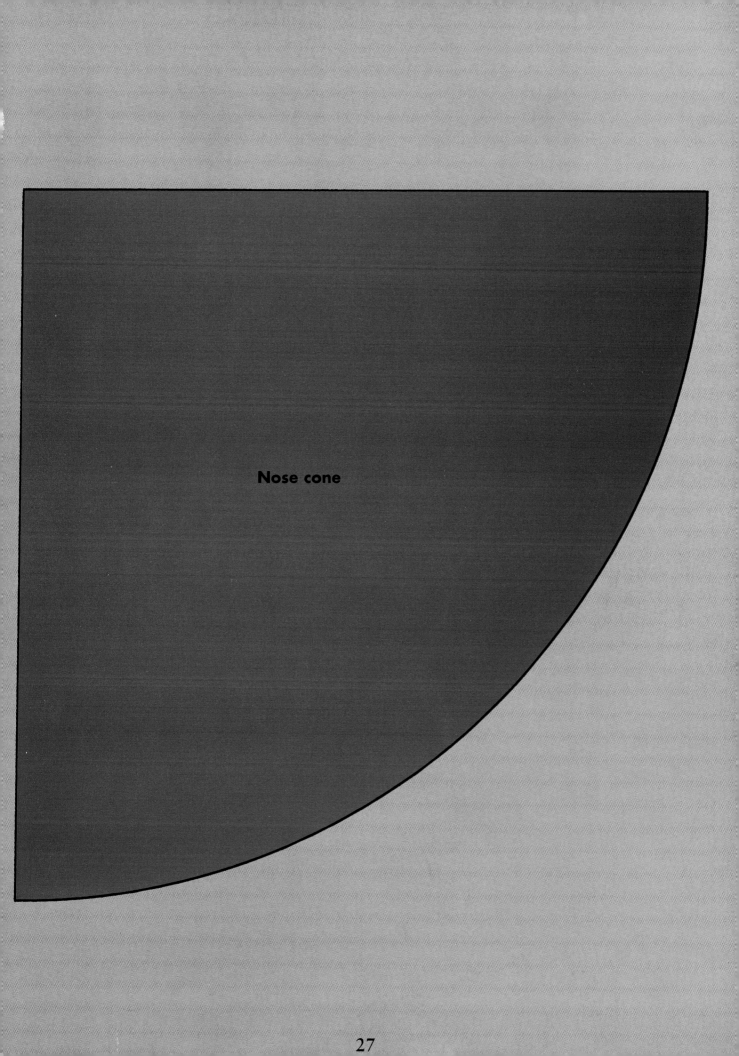

Nose cone

CHAPTER 2—CARS, TRAINS, MOTORCYCLES

THE SCIENCE OF MOTION

Steam engines were the first form of power for vehicles. This steam car appeared in 1854.

Land vehicles are like all moving objects. To move, they must accelerate (speed up), decelerate (slow down), and keep their speed. They often need to change direction, too. But they will only change speed or direction when a force acts on them. In vehicles, these forces come from the engine, brakes, and wheels.

THE FORCES ON A VEHICLE

Several different forces act on a vehicle as it moves. Thrust is the force created by the engine that pushes the vehicle forward. Two forces act in the opposite direction. They are drag, created by the air flowing past the vehicle as it moves, and friction, which tries to stop the vehicle's moving parts from sliding against each other.

Thrust created by the engine drives the vehicle forward.

CONTROLS

Electronic systems make vehicles safer and cheaper. They include anti-lock braking, engine management, and navigation systems.

Because of gravity's pull the vehicle needs more power to go uphill than downhill. It also presses the tires onto the road.

BODY AND STRUCTURE

A vehicle needs a solid structure to support its heavy mechanical parts. A strong body also helps to protect passengers from injury (*right*).

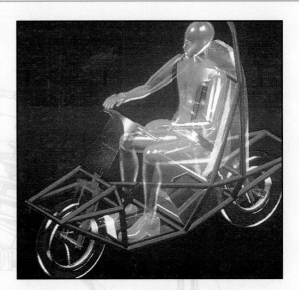

Drag slows down a moving vehicle.

Friction in the wheel bearings slows a vehicle down.

Gravity pulls the vehicle downward.

ENGINES AND MOTORS

Most vehicles have gasoline engines, where the fuel burns inside cylinders. The engine releases the energy stored in the fuel and uses it to make the vehicle move. Electric trains and some cars have electric motors instead of gasoline engines.

Model car project box

To make the projects, you will need: thick and thin cardboard, corrugated cardboard, rubber bands, a craft knife, scissors, white glue, strong clear glue, paper clips, acrylic paint, a felt tip pen case, beads, wooden dowel, a bendy drinking straw, stapler and staples, thin wire, and tinfoil.

Science experiment project box

WHEELS

Wheels let a vehicle roll smoothly along. Their tires create friction with the road, causing traction (grip) for acceleration and for braking. Some trains are held clear of their tracks with magnets (*left*). This removes all friction with the rails.

WHEELS

Friction is very important for vehicle designers. It is a force that tries to stop surfaces from moving against each other. A vehicle without wheels would create huge friction between itself and the ground. This would make it very difficult to move.

WHAT IS FRICTION?

Friction happens between two surfaces because bumps and hollows in the surfaces catch against each other. Even  smooth surfaces look quite rough under a microscope (*above*).

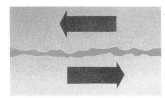 When slippery liquids, called lubricants, are put between the two surfaces, they separate them slightly. This stops the bumps from catching and reduces the friction. Moving parts in vehicles are usually lubricated with oil.

Another way of reducing friction is to put balls or cylinders between the surfaces. Only a small part of each ball touches the surfaces at one time, and this reduces friction.

AXLES AND BEARINGS

Wheels are firmly attached to a vehicle with an axle or a shaft. These help the wheels to turn freely because they are much thinner than a wheel—so there is a smaller surface to create friction.

The axle is supported inside a ring by balls. These reduce friction because they touch only a small part of the axle's surface.

Ball bearing

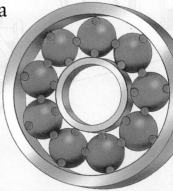

WHY WHEELS WORK

Wheels reduce friction because they roll with the movement of the vehicle, without any surfaces rubbing together. At the same time, they provide grip because of the friction between the tire and the road.

Maglev (short for magnetic levitation) trains are pushed clear of their tracks by magnets, which reduces the friction to zero.

Magnets

Magnets

TRAIN WHEELS

A train wheel is a solid steel disk. Wheels come in pairs on steel rods called axles. The axles are attached to the train with bearings. Each wheel has a lip (or flange) on the inside rim to stop it from slipping sideways off its rail.

Flange

MODEL CAR
PART 1
WHEELS

Add a rubber band to make tires

1 To make your car, start with the wheels. Trace eight part **A**s from the plans on pages 50-51. Then cut them out from corrugated cardboard.

2 Glue two part **A**s together to make a front wheel. To make a back wheel, straighten out one half of a paper clip and poke it through a part **A**. Then glue another part **A** to it (*right*). Make two back wheels and two front wheels in all.

3 Cut a piece of dowel so that it is just wider than part **M** (see page 51). Then glue a front wheel to one end.

4 For the axle, roll up a piece of cardboard so that it fits around the dowel, then glue it (*below*). Thread the dowel through and glue the other front wheel to it.

Dowel fits in here

SUSPENSION AND TIRES

If a vehicle's wheels were attached firmly to its body, the passengers would feel every bump that the vehicle went over. A suspension system allows the wheels to move up and down under the body, reducing the effect of the bumps.

To feel how a spring works, hop up then land without bending your knees. Can you feel the force? That's why you normally bend your knees, because they act like springs to give you a soft landing.

With a simple spring suspension, the vehicle would keep bouncing after going over a bump. A device called a damper prevents this.

Make your own springs

Leaf spring

3. Oil stops spring from bouncing back.

SPRINGS

When a spring is squashed, it stores energy, then releases it when it bounces back. Some springs are coils, others are made of curved plates of metal (called leaf springs). These work like a diving board, but bend in the middle.

A spring also bounces back if it is stretched.

A spring shape will only work if it is made from an "elastic" material—one that returns to its original shape after being squashed or stretched.

AIR SUSPENSION

Some vehicles use air suspension. Instead of metal springs, air is squashed and expands inside a sealed cylinder.

Air

2. After landing, the spring is squashed.

1. Before landing, spring is at its normal length.

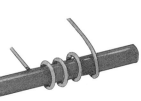

MODEL CAR
PART 2
SUSPENSION

1 To make a spring, coil some thin wire around a pen four times (*left*). Then make five more springs like this one.

2 Cut out part **B** from thick cardboard, including the hole for the steering wheel (marked **C**). Stick two springs at positions **D** and **E**. Then glue **B** to the front axle section you made on page 31.

3 Cut out part **F** from thick cardboard and stick the other four springs onto it at positions **G**, **H**, **I**, and **J**, using strong glue.

SHOCK ABSORBERS

A shock absorber is a cylinder filled with thick oil that surrounds a piston connected to the wheel. After a spring is squashed going over a bump, the thick oil slows the piston down and stops the spring from bouncing back.

TIRES

A modern tire is made up of many layers. Inside is a tube filled with air that acts like a spring. The outside of the tire normally has a pattern of grooves. In wet weather, these stop the vehicle from slipping by letting water escape from between the tire and the road.

Wet weather tires

Racing cars use tires with no tread in dry conditions.

Rubber tread

Rayon

Steel band

Wire

STRUCTURE

A car's body creates a space for the passengers and their luggage or cargo, and normally supports all the other parts of the car. The body needs to be a strong structure that protects the passengers and is rigid enough to support the weight of the engine.

It must also be as light as possible to let the car speed up and slow down quickly.

You can test how a car's crumple zone works. See the experiment on page 35.

Until the 1940s, most cars had a heavy metal chassis that supported the wheels and engine. The body, called coachwork, was built on top. This was often made from wood.

Chassis

 MODEL CAR
PART 3

THE BODY

1 Cut out the body (part **K**) from thin cardboard. Don't forget to cut out the hole for the steering (**L**). Then glue the body together using the tabs.

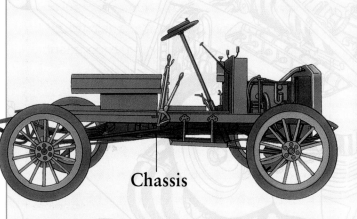

L

K

M

N

2 Then cut out the base (part **M**) from thick cardboard. Next, cut out the hole for the steering (**N**). You have now made the main sections—turn to page 39 to add the power!

MOTORCYCLES AND TRAINS

A motorcycle frame is made of metal tubes welded together to create a strong but light structure that supports all the other parts of the bike.

Trains are built more like old cars, with the body and engine sitting on a heavy chassis.

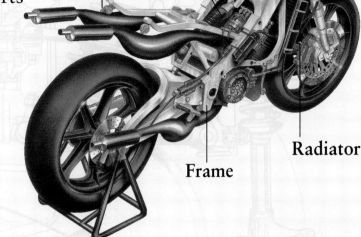

Exhaust Engine

Radiator

Frame

Monocoque structure

BODY SHELLS

Most cars are built around a single-piece metal shell called a monocoque. This is made from sheets of metal pressed into shape and welded together. Other body panels are connected to the shell by bolts and hinges.

Crumple Zones

Crumple zones are sections of a car's body that collapse in a collision, reducing the force of the impact. To see how they work, try this experiment.

1 Find a rectangular box. At one end, tape on a sheet of paper (or two) to make a tube. This makes a rigid crumple zone.

Add a shoe for extra weight

2 Drop the box onto a hard surface on the solid end and it will bounce after the hard impact. Now drop the box on its crumple zone, and the impact is absorbed as the tube crumples up.

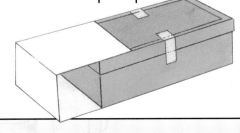

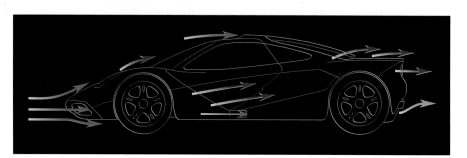

AIR FLOW

The more easily the air can flow around a vehicle, the smaller the drag on the vehicle. A car with good streamlining will go faster and use less fuel than a badly designed one.

STREAMLINING

Drag is the force that tries to slow a vehicle as it moves through the air. The faster the vehicle goes, the greater the drag gets. In fact, if the speed doubles, the drag becomes four times greater.

Eventually, drag gets as big as the thrust from the engine, stopping the vehicle from going any faster.

Streamlining is shaping the vehicle's body to reduce drag.

You can use a model car to test streamlining and drag for yourself.

SMOOTH TRAINS

Streamlining is important for all vehicles. High-speed express trains need careful streamlining at the front. Curved shapes allow the air in front of the train to flow smoothly over, under, and around it.

HIGH-SPEED CARS

City cars hardly ever reach high speeds, so streamlining is less important than it is for cars designed for high-speed highway travel. Racing cars also have airfoils, parts that are shaped like a plane's wing. They push the car down, increasing its grip on the road.

Formula 1 car

airfoil   airfoil

A racing bike has smooth body panels for extra speed.

The smooth shape of these modern city cars helps them to use less fuel.

Streamlining

Try this experiment to test streamlining.

1 Take an old toy car and drop it down the sloping end of a full bath (*bottom*). Place a coin on the bottom of the bath to mark how far it goes.

2 Then find a small, rectangular cardboard box that covers the outside of the car. Tape it over the car, then try sliding the car down the bath again. It won't go as far, because its shape is less streamlined.

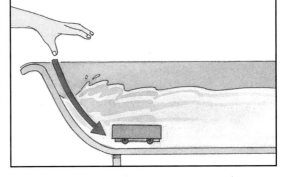

Motorcycles have a smooth front section called a fairing. This guides the air around the motorcycle. The rider can duck behind it to reduce drag, too.

ENGINES

A vehicle's engine provides the energy needed to move the vehicle. The job of the engine is to convert the chemical energy stored in fuel into energy that makes the vehicle move.

It does this by burning fuel. This turns chemical energy into heat energy. The heat energy makes the burning gases expand inside a cylinder. The gases push against a piston, which turns the crankshaft.

The main picture shows how a single cylinder works. But most engines have from two to eight cylinders.

Camshaft

Valves

Exhaust out

Spark plug

Piston

Crankshaft

Power from Chemicals

In an engine, the pistons are moved by hot gases. These are created during a chemical reaction between fuel and air. In this experiment, gas released from chemicals is used to force your hands apart.

1 Pour four teaspoons of baking soda into an empty plastic bottle and fold the bottle tightly in half.

2 Pour a few teaspoons of vinegar into the bottle and put the top on. Squeeze the bottle between your hands and shake it to mix the chemicals. The reaction creates gas that fills the bottle, forcing your hands apart (*top*).

The crankshaft is linked to the camshaft by a chain or belt. As it turns, the camshaft opens the valves that let fuel and air get into the pistons and exhaust gases get out.

INSIDE A GASOLINE ENGINE

In a gasoline engine, fuel mixed with air burns inside the cylinders. The fuel burns in short bursts, making explosions that create hot gases. The gases push the pistons, which are linked to the transmission by the crankshaft. Waste gases are pushed out of the car through the exhaust system.

The mix of fuel and air is lit by a tiny spark from a spark plug (*left*) powered by electricity.

—— Carburetor

Air in

Pipe from fuel tank

Fuel in

FUEL AND AIR MIX

Fuel cannot burn without oxygen from the air. So it is mixed with air inside the carburetor before being sucked into the pistons.

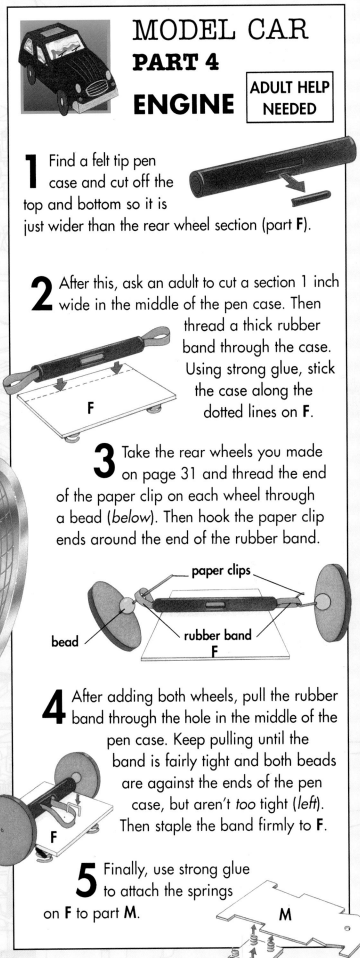

MODEL CAR
PART 4
ENGINE

ADULT HELP NEEDED

1 Find a felt tip pen case and cut off the top and bottom so it is just wider than the rear wheel section (part **F**).

2 After this, ask an adult to cut a section 1 inch wide in the middle of the pen case. Then thread a thick rubber band through the case. Using strong glue, stick the case along the dotted lines on **F**.

F

3 Take the rear wheels you made on page 31 and thread the end of the paper clip on each wheel through a bead (*below*). Then hook the paper clip ends around the end of the rubber band.

paper clips

bead

rubber band

F

4 After adding both wheels, pull the rubber band through the hole in the middle of the pen case. Keep pulling until the band is fairly tight and both beads are against the ends of the pen case, but aren't *too* tight (*left*). Then staple the band firmly to **F**.

F

5 Finally, use strong glue to attach the springs on **F** to part **M**.

M

OTHER ENGINES

Most cars are powered by gasoline engines. But other types of engine are increasingly common. Diesel engines are often used in trucks, and electric motors are used in many trains.

Some engines are also designed to use unusual fuels, such as methane or hydrogen. A few high-speed, record-breaking cars have used jet or rocket engines.

You can feel how the air and fuel inside a diesel engine heat up as they are squashed. Feel how a bicycle pump heats up as you pump up a tire.

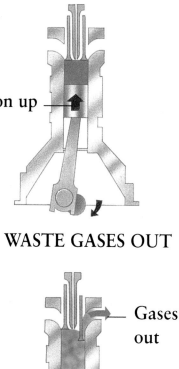

Gasoline engine

1 AIR SUCKED IN

Air in →

Piston down

2 PISTON SQUASHES AIR

Piston up

3 FUEL IS LIT

Fuel in and explodes

Piston down

4 WASTE GASES OUT

Gases out

Piston up

Crankshaft

THE DIESEL ENGINE

In a diesel engine, air inside the cylinders is compressed (squashed) by the pistons. This makes the air very hot.

Fuel is injected into the air, which is so hot that the thick diesel fuel explodes. This pushes the pistons down and drives the crankshaft around.

ELECTRIC MOTORS

An electric motor turns electrical energy into movement (kinetic energy). Inside the motor, a coil of wire, called a rotor, has magnets around it. When electricity flows through the rotor, the magnets make it spin. The electrical energy comes from batteries, where it is stored as chemical energy. But most electric cars can only travel a short distance before their batteries need charging again.

Magnet

Magnet   Rotor   Electricity supply

HYBRID CARS

Some cars have a gasoline engine *and* electric motors on each wheel. Batteries provide the electricity for the motors on short journeys.

On long journeys, where the batteries would run down, the engine drives a generator that produces electricity for the motors.

Electric motor

Electric locomotives get power from overhead electric cables, from a third electric rail on the track, or from a generator driven by a diesel engine.

Electric cables

ELECTRIC MOTOR

Electricity supply

Rotor

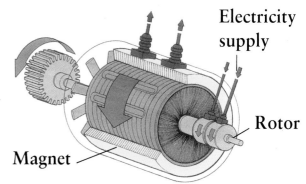

Battery

Motors

Magnet

CONTROLS

A driver uses simple controls (accelerator, clutch, and brake pedals, a gear shift, and a steering wheel) to make a car speed up, slow down, and turn.

Many modern cars have complex electronic circuits that help the driver to drive safely and in comfort.

Add steering to your model.

TODAY'S CAR

We are just entering a new age where we have huge control over our car. In the first cars, levers and springs were used to apply controls. The latest cars combine computers and hydraulics.

Modern cars are also increasingly "green." Filters such as CATS (catalytic converters) help cut out harmful exhaust gases that pollute the atmosphere.

The Mercedes A class, shown here, has a computer that makes the most efficient use of fuel at different speeds and controls the car's braking and balance.

Navigation

Stabilizing controls

Computer

Fuel injection

Anti-lock brakes

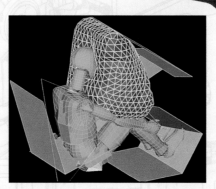

If a car stops violently, air bags inflate quickly to stop passengers from going through the windshield.

Air-conditioning systems keep the air inside the car at a comfortable temperature and humidity.

THE BEST ROUTE

In-car navigation systems guide drivers automatically to their destinations. They use a satellite navigation system to determine where the car is, and a database of roads to determine the best route. Some systems can also receive information about traffic jams and navigate around them.

NOT TOO CLOSE!

Some of the newest cars have a detection system that warns the driver if they are too close to the car in front, and applies the brakes to prevent the car from getting any closer.

A similar system warns the driver about objects in the way when the car is in reverse.

Power steering

Exhaust system

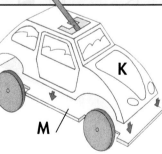

MODEL CAR
PART 5
STEERING

1 Push a bendy drinking straw through the holes in **M** and **B** and glue it to **B**. Cut out **O**, and glue this to the straw above **M** so that the springs on the front axle touch **M**, but **B** can still turn freely.

Drinking straw

M

O

K

M

Front wheel section

B

2 Now glue **K** to **M**. The straw should poke out of the top of **K**. Try the straw in different slots to steer the car.

GEAR SYSTEMS

A car's transmission system carries the power from the engine to the wheels. It is made up of a gearbox (and normally a clutch) and driveshafts. The faster the engine turns, the more power it produces. Gears allow the engine to turn quickly whether the car is just starting off or speeding along.

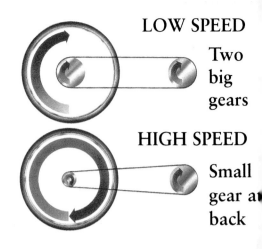

LOW SPEED
Two big gears

HIGH SPEED
Small gear at back

Two gears the same size spin at the same speed. But if one gear is twice as big as the other, the small gear will spin twice as fast.

Gearshift

Gear wheels

Crankshaft from engine

TRANSMISSION

The crankshaft leads to the transmission, where its speed is reduced by the gear. The gearshift selects a set of gears that make the correct reduction for the car's speed. First gear makes the wheels turn very slowly for starting off. Higher gears make the wheels turn more quickly for driving. The clutch releases the gears from the engine. This allows a smooth change from one gear to another.

THE DIFFERENTIAL

The differential allows a pair of wheels being driven by the engine to turn at different speeds as a car turns a corner.

When a car drives straight, the small differential gears are carried around by the crown wheel. When a car turns corners, the differential gears spin the two driveshafts at different speeds.

Driveshaft to wheel

Crown wheel

Differential gearwheel

Differential gearwheel

Driveshaft from transmission

Driveshaft to wheel

When a car goes around a tight corner, the wheels on the outside of the corner have to travel farther than those on the inside.

Spur gears

TYPES OF GEARS

Gear mechanisms are used to transfer power, normally from one spinning shaft to another. They can change the speed and direction of the rotation.

Spur gears are used when the shafts are parallel to each other. Bevel gears connect shafts at right angles. Rack and pinion gears connect a shaft with a straight surface that moves from side to side.

Bevel gears

Rack and pinion gears

CHANGING SPEED AND DIRECTION

To accelerate, a vehicle needs more thrust. This is achieved by sending more fuel to the engine. To slow down, it needs more friction. This is achieved by using the brakes to increase the friction on the wheels. To steer around a curve, a vehicle needs a force acting on it toward the bend. In a car, this force comes from the friction of tires pushing sideways against the road.

Slide a ruler between your thumb and finger (*above right*). The tighter you grip the ruler, the greater the friction. This is how brakes work.

BRAKES

Brakes work by pressing pads against parts of the wheels. This creates friction that slows the wheels. But if the driver presses too hard on the brake pedal, especially on wet roads, the brakes "lock," making the wheels skid (*above*). An anti-lock braking system (ABS) detects if the wheels are about to skid and releases the brakes slightly.

In drum brakes, each wheel has a drum attached and brake pads press on its inside.

Drum

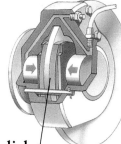

Brake disk

In disk brakes, each wheel has a metal disk attached and brake pads press on each side of it.

AROUND THE BEND

Because trains run on tracks, the engineer does not need to steer. The force to make the train go around a curve comes from the track pushing sideways on the wheels. If a train turned too quickly, this force would tip it over. Tilting the train (or the track) helps to prevent this.

Motorcyclists lean over as they turn corners. This stops the sideways force on the tires from flipping the bike sideways.

The spinning wheels create a force at right angles to the bike.

Gravity pulls downward

Spin Power
The gyroscopic effect of the spinning wheels helps motorcycles and bicycles stay upright when they are moving.
   The same effect stops a spinning top from toppling over. Try making a top from a short pencil and circle of cardboard.

Forces at right angles to the spin

Racing car steering system

CAR STEERING

A normal car steering system uses a gear system called a rack and pinion to change the turning motion of the steering wheel into a sideways movement that twists the wheels from side to side. Turn to page 45 to see the special gears used for this.

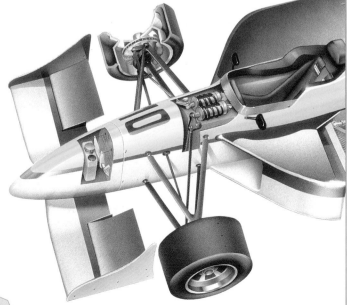

IN A COLLISION

Any moving object keeps on moving at the same speed unless something stops it or slows it down. This is what we call momentum.

If a car comes to a sudden stop, the driver and passengers continue to move because of this momentum. Only seat belts stop them from being thrown toward the front of the car.

KEEPING SAFE

A huge amount of research goes into making vehicles safer for travel. Vehicles have two types of safety systems— systems that help to prevent accidents, and systems that protect passengers if an accident occurs.

Emergency telephone

This new-style motorcycle has a lightweight, weatherproof body that protects the driver from wind and rain. The body is streamlined to reduce drag.

SIGNAL FOR SAFETY

Preventing collisions is especially important on railroads, where a single train can carry hundred of passengers. Complex electronic circuits operate signals and switches. Automatic train protection systems on the trains themselves apply the brakes if the driver goes past a red light

MODEL CAR
PART 6
PAINTING

1 Finish your car by painting it and adding pieces of tinfoil for the headlights.

2 To drive the car, wind up the rubber band by rolling the car backward along the floor.

The latest display systems project signs onto the inside of the windshield, where the driver can read them without looking away from the road.

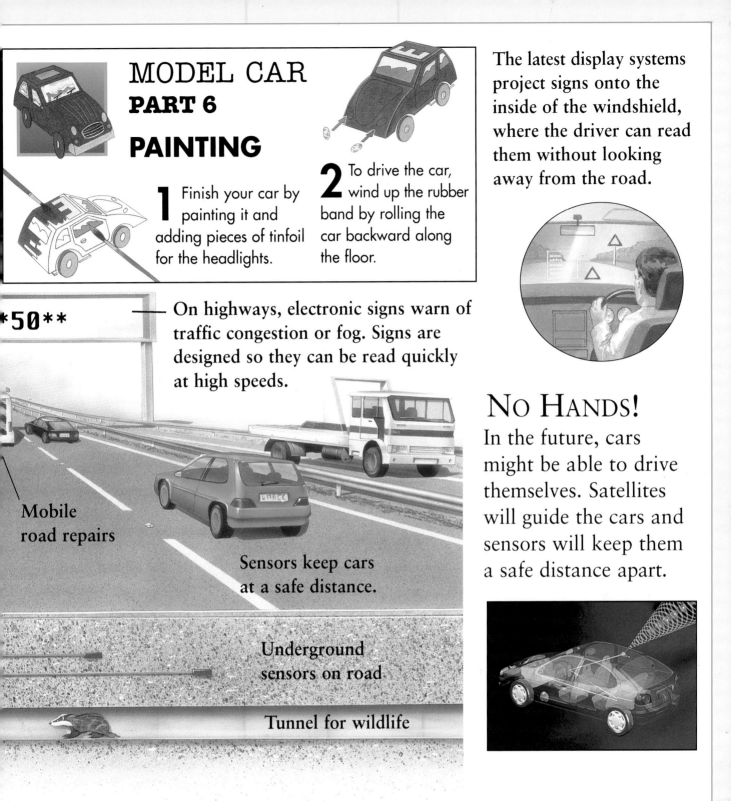

*50**

On highways, electronic signs warn of traffic congestion or fog. Signs are designed so they can be read quickly at high speeds.

Mobile road repairs

Sensors keep cars at a safe distance.

Underground sensors on road

Tunnel for wildlife

NO HANDS!

In the future, cars might be able to drive themselves. Satellites will guide the cars and sensors will keep them a safe distance apart.

DIFFICULT DRIVING

Bad weather, such as heavy rain, can make driving dangerous. Windshield wipers give the driver a better view and temperature sensors warns drivers that ice is likely to form on the road.

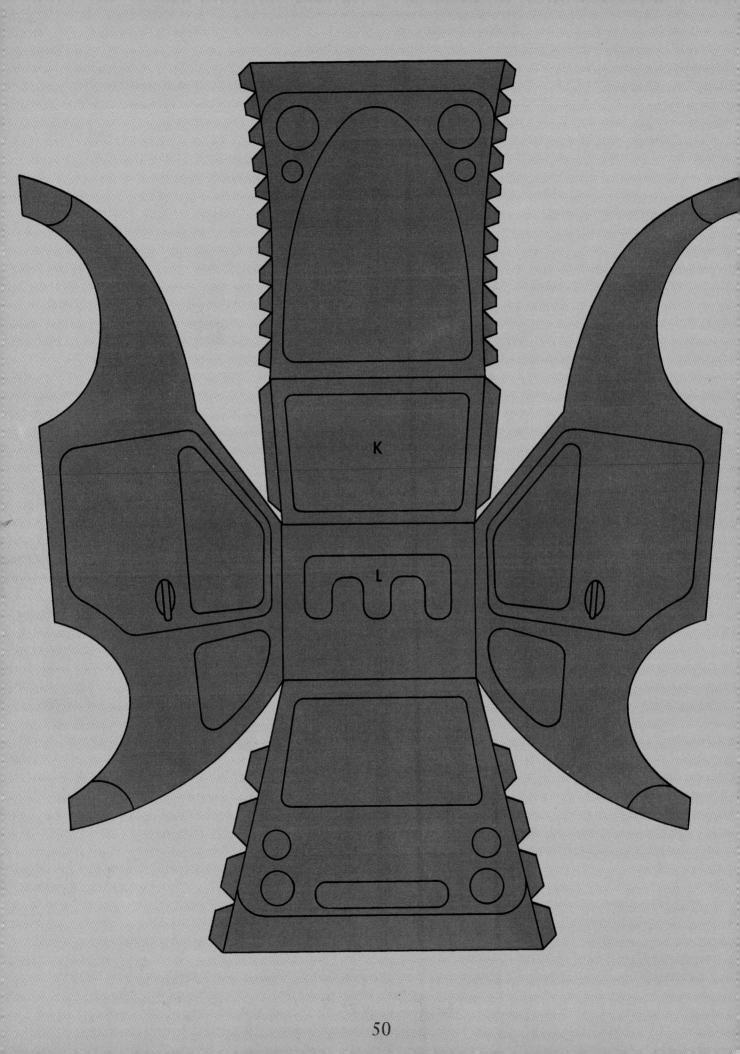

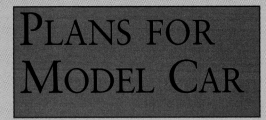

PLANS FOR MODEL CAR

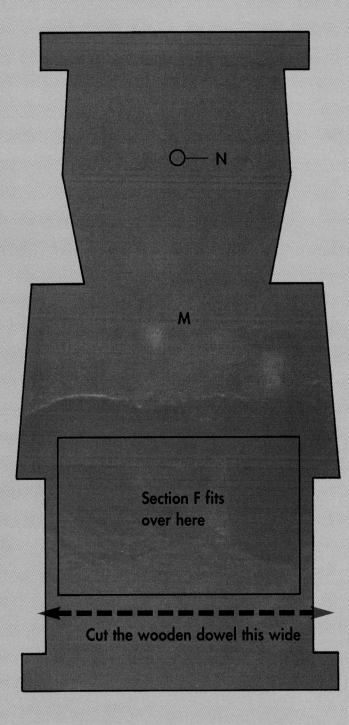

N

M

Section F fits
over here

Cut the wooden dowel this wide

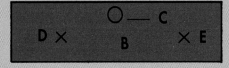

D ×   O — C   × E
B

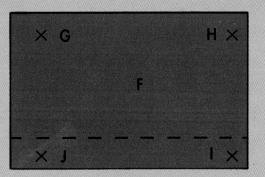

× G   H ×

F

× J   I ×

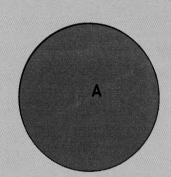

A

Canoe

The first boats were logs roped together. Later, logs or bark were hollowed out to make canoes (*above*). But they weren't much use in rough seas.

Roman galley

The bow is the front of a ship, the stern is the back.

Sails were used on most long journeys from about 3000 BC until the invention of steam power.

CHAPTER 3—SEACRAFT
THE SCIENCE OF FLOATING

Millions of years ago, early humans used boats to spread around the world. Since then, designers have learned a lot about what makes a good boat. But some things haven't changed. Ships must float, they work best with a strong, smooth shape, and they need something to push or pull them through the water.

A lifeboat (*right*) has to be well designed. It needs to stay afloat and travel quickly in the roughest seas.

POWER

Paddling is the simplest way to move a boat. The Romans used oars, which used leverage to provide more power. With the invention of steam power in the 18th century, paddles (*right*) and then propellers were used to propel ships.

SHAPE

A ship's shape keeps it afloat. But a designer must also decide between a shape that has the most space for cargo, and a shape that slips easily through the water. Broader ships carry more; slimmer ships go faster as they produce less drag.

The right side of a ship is called starboard, the left side is called port.

MATERIALS

Any material that is strong and can be made into the right shape is suitable for a hull. Reeds and animal skins were used in the earliest times. Today, steel, plastic, fiberglass, and wood are used.

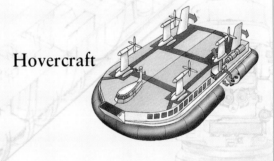

Hovercraft

Not all seacraft have hulls like a ship. Hovercraft (*above*) float on a cushion of air trapped inside a giant "skirt." Submarines (*below*) sink as well as float. But because they travel underwater, they need a very strong, smooth shape.

Model boat project box

Science experiment project box

To make the projects, you will need: a plastic bottle, empty fruit juice cartons, paper, cardboard, scissors, tape and craft glue, a ruler, a pencil, modeling clay, marbles, oil-based paints, rubber bands, straws, coins, tinfoil, a balloon, and some flexible wire.

Submarine

SHAPE

Many ships are made of heavy steel. So how do they float? Any object placed in water weighs less than it does in air, because it displaces water (pushes it out of the way). The water pushes back with a force equal to the weight of water displaced. Wood floats because it weighs less than the water it displaces. Steel ships float because a hull shape increases the amount of water they displace.

SS Great Eastern

THE HULL SHAPE

A steel raft sinks because it weighs more than the water it displaces. A steel hull shape takes up more space, increasing the upward push of water.

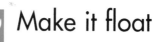

A hull takes up more space than a raft because of the air inside the hull shape.

Propulsion is the force driving a ship forward.

The upward push of water keeps a ship afloat.

Make it float

1 If you drop a solid lump of modeling clay into water, it sinks.
2 Now roll the modeling clay flat. Then curl up the edges to make a boat shape. **3** Gently place your boat into a bowl filled with water. It should float.
4 Add marbles to your boat. Mark your own plimsoll line on the side to show where your boat can be filled without danger of it tipping over.

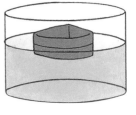

3

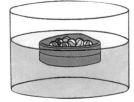

4

1

2

WONDERFUL WOOD

Most wood is a good material for ships because it floats whatever its shape. It is also strong enough to cope with the many forces acting on a hull.

BALLAST

A ship can be too light. Have you ever seen how a cork bobs on the surface of the water? To prevent this, empty ships carry extra weight in their hull, called ballast. Seawater is often used as ballast as it can be pumped out when the ship takes on cargo.

Trimarans (boats with three hulls) are quite stable without much ballast.

The weight of a ship pushes downward.

Drag is the resistance of the water pushed aside by the hull as a ship moves through the water. Turn over to find out more.

5

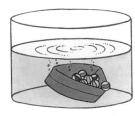

5 Test your design in rough seas by shaking the side of the bowl. Is your boat overloaded?

PLIMSOLL LINE

Many 19th-century cargo ships sank because they were overloaded. In 1876, politician Samuel Plimsoll gave his name to the line which, by law, then had to be drawn on the side of British ships to mark the safe loading level (*right*).

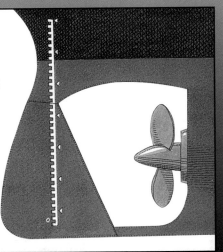

DEALING WITH DRAG

The shape of a ship's hull also affects its speed. Slim hulls create less drag than broad ones. That means that long ships are best, because they combine plenty of space with minimum drag. The ultimate racing shape is the boat used by rowing eights. They are lightweight and needle-thin—but are easily sunk in rough water.

Adding outriggers

The thin hull of this yacht (*left*) creates less drag as the water flows smoothly around it.

This 15th-century ship (*right*) had a wide hull to make it stable in rough seas. But its shape creates more drag, as the water does not flow so smoothly around it.

The flow of water around thin (*above*) and wide (*below*) hulls

HULLS FOR SPEED

Monohull

Fast speedboats reduce drag by "flying" on the surface of the water rather than plowing through it. They have flattish bottoms to make them skim along like surfboards. Catamarans go fast because their two slim hulls create less drag than one fat one (monohull).

The fastest speed boats are catamarans.

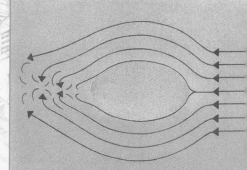

Catamaran

HOVERCRAFT

A hovercraft (*above*) avoids most drag by floating on a cushion of air. Its large fans suck air in and force it underneath the craft. The air is then held in place by a flexible skirt that allows the hovercraft to travel on land and water.

Hydrofoil

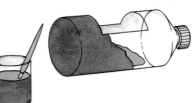

HYDROFOILS

A hydrofoil has underwater wings mounted on its hull (*above*). As it moves faster, these wings create a lifting force like an aircraft's wing. They push the hull out of the water, reducing the drag.

Crossbow

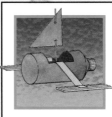

MODEL BOAT
PART 1

THE HULL

1 Take a 20-oz plastic bottle with the top screwed on and cut a hole in one side. Plastic is a good material for a small boat as it is both light and waterproof. The long, thin shape of the bottle won't create too much drag.

2 It's best to decorate your ship's hull now before adding the other parts. In real boats, painting plays an important role. Wooden boats are often painted with oily tar that seals the cracks in the planks. Metal boats are covered in a paint that stops them from rusting.

3 Your round bottle would spin around if you left it as it is. So build two outriggers for extra balance, using part **A** from the plans on page 74. Cut two part **A**s from a juice carton, then fold them into an L-shape along the dotted lines.

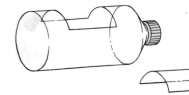

4 Next, glue four straws together to make the floats. Glue the floats to part **A**, then glue this to the bottle. Outriggers are often used to stabilize boats with a thin main hull, such as the sailing speed record holder, *Crossbow* (*left*).

STAYING AFLOAT

The hull also needs to be watertight. In the past, boats were coated in tar to prevent leaks. Today's metal hulls can rust, creating small holes for water to get in. However, watertight compartments allow a ship to stay afloat even if one section is flooded.

Surf boats (*above*) are so light they won't sink even when they are almost full of water.

KEEPING THE WATER OUT

In a rough sea, waves sweep over the decks of even giant tankers (*above*), but decks and hatches seal off the interior. Car ferries also have huge bow doors to let cars in. If the doors aren't closed properly, they can sink in minutes.

Modern ships have high-speed pumps to pump out ballast water from the bilges or to pump up seawater in case of fire.

UNSINKABLE?

The *RMS Titanic* (*below*) was supposed to be unsinkable because it was built with a series of watertight compartments. But an iceberg ripped such a long tear in its hull that it sank anyway (*above*).

RMS Titanic

TO THE RESCUE

Small boats that have to brave the wildest seas are designed to be truly unsinkable. Heroic rescues were once made in open rowboats, but lifeboats today are sturdy boats with fiberglass hulls designed to right themselves if they are turned over.

The *Atlantic 21* (*right*) has an airbag to turn it upright.

Arun class lifeboat (*below*)

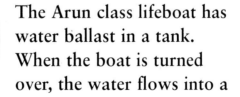

The Arun class lifeboat has water ballast in a tank. When the boat is turned over, the water flows into a righting tank on one side of the boat. This creates a force that turns the boat upright again (*below*).

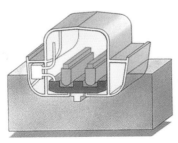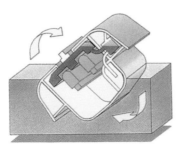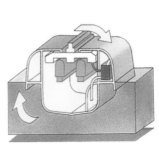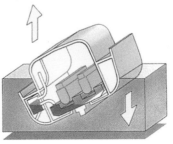

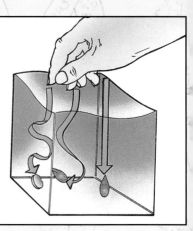

SUBMARINES

Some ships are actually meant to sink—submarines! Most are designed for use in war, to attack ships on the surface or to fire long-range missiles. To stay hidden, modern submarines can stay underwater for months at a time. Their engines and propellers are designed to be as quiet as possible.

Turtle

Submarines are shaped like orcas.

Outer hull | Turbine | Nuclear reactor

Inner hull

SHAPE

Submarines are fast, capable of 30 knots or more, and have a smooth shape for low drag. The teardrop shape of the 18th-century *Turtle* (*above*) was good for sinking, but today's long, slim hull is better for speed.

Trieste

Research submarines have strong hulls to withstand the huge pressures at the bottom of the ocean. The *Trieste* was used to explore the depths of the Pacific Ocean. It reached a depth of over 35,797 feet in the Marianas Trench.

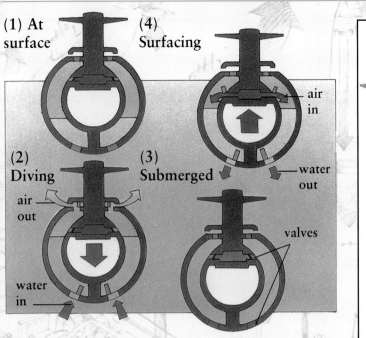

(1) At surface

(4) Surfacing

air in

(2) Diving

air out

water in

(3) Submerged

water out

valves

To dive, valves are opened to allow sea water to flood the ballast tanks between the two hulls. Air is allowed to escape as the water comes in (2). To surface, compressed air stored onboard is used to blow the water out of the tanks again (4).

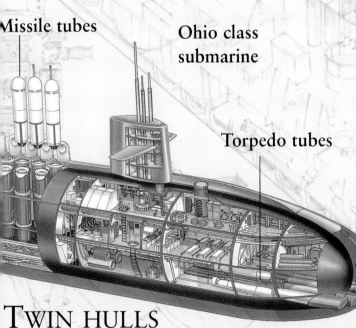

Missile tubes

Ohio class submarine

Torpedo tubes

TWIN HULLS

A submarine has two hulls. The inner, pressure hull protects it from the crushing force of water at great depths. The outer hull fits around it and contains the ballast tanks.

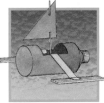

Submarine project

1 Make a submarine from a plastic soda bottle. First, carefully cut three holes on one side. If you want to paint your submarine, it's best to do it now.

2 Next, attach coins near the three holes with lumps of modeling clay. The coins act as ballast (*above*). Then attach a straw into the top hole with modeling clay, making a watertight fit. Seal the other end of the straw with tape or clay.

3 Now place your vessel in water. It should stay upright—if not, add more ballast. Then take the tape off the end of the straw. This is the same as opening the vents to dive on a real submarine. Air rushes out of the bottle, water rushes in, and the submarine dives. To bring your submarine back to the surface, blow into the straw to push out the water (*below* and *above left*).

STRUCTURE

Modern ships are mostly built of steel. Metal plates and girders are welded together to make boxlike sections. These sections are joined and the ship is divided into separate watertight compartments. Wood is one of the best materials for ships as it floats. Dug-out canoes are limited by the size of the tree trunk from which they are made, but large ships can be made from wood.

BUILDING FROM WOOD

Wooden boats are made by bending planks called strakes around the frame. To make them bend easily, they are first softened in a steam-filled box. Nails hold them together.

The planks can be joined to one another, to form a smooth round shape.

Or the planks can be overlapped, forming a clinker boat, like a longship.

Or they can be laid at angles to each other, forming a chine hull.

A Viking longship was built by:
1 Making the central keel.
2 Adding the side planks.
3 Joining planks running along and across for extra strength.
4 Making a strong support for the mast.

FIBERGLASS BOATS

Plastic is also an excellent material for boats. It is light, waterproof—and not attacked by worms! To make it stronger, it is reinforced by fine fibers of glass. To make a boat, fiberglass mats are laid over a mold (*right*) then cured by coating them with resin, which sets hard.

VIKING BOATS

Wooden boats are still built around a frame (*above*). The basic shape hasn't changed much since the longship used by Vikings a thousand years ago (*left*). In fact, some of the tools haven't changed much, either.

3

4

Clinker project

1 You can build a clinker hull using the plans on page 74. First, cut out fourteen planks (**B**) and two end (**C**) parts from stiff cardboard.

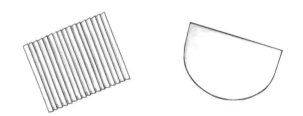

2 Next, glue the planks together (*above*), overlapping one on top of the other. Before the glue has fully set, bend the planks around to form a semicircle shape. Then glue the end sections onto the tabs (formed by folding the planks on the dotted lines).

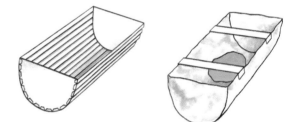

3 To add strength and to make the hull watertight, wrap it in tinfoil. Finally, add clay to the bottom as ballast (*above*). Use this hull as an alternative in later sections.

HOW MANY SAILS?

The big sailing ships of the 19th century had three or more masts, and six sails to each mast. The more sails, the faster they could go. But they needed large crews to manage them.

Modern yachts usually have one mast and up to six sails for different conditions.

Sails shaped like rotors also use air pressure.

If you blow into your model sail, feel the force as the mast pulls away from you.

Extra sails can speed up the air flowing around the back of the main sail by squeezing it into the gap between them. This adds to the force on the main sail.

POWER

Before steam engines, sails were the best way to propel a boat. Early ships used square sails that caught the wind from behind, but they couldn't sail into the wind. Later, yachts set their sails at an angle. Set like this, sails use air pressure in a different way, and allow a boat to sail into the wind.

3 Boat moves forward

Keels

Instead of using outriggers, you can balance your model with a keel. Cut out a wedge-shaped piece (part **E**) from a fruit juice carton. Then fix a lump of modeling clay to each end and stick one end to your boat's bottom.

The weight on the end of a keel helps to keep a boat upright, while the force of the water pushing against it stops the boat from going sideways.

Air flowing over sails gives them a curved, airfoil shape. The sails act like the wings of a plane, creating forces that make the yacht lean over, and move forward. The keel and the weight of the crew stop the boat from capsizing, unless the wind is very strong.

MODEL BOAT
PART 2

ADDING SAILS

1 Cut a triangular piece of paper to make a sail (part **D**). Then pierce two holes in it, one above the other, to thread your mast through. Anchor the mast to the bottom of the boat using modeling clay.

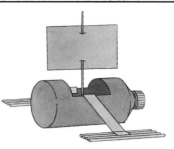

2 Try the same thing with a square sail (*above*). Does this work as well as the triangular sail when you blow from the side?

1 Wind travels faster around the far edge of the sail, creating low pressure.

Wind

2 The higher pressure on the near side pushes the sail forward. The keel stops the boat from moving sideways.

No boat can sail directly toward the wind. But by setting its sails nearly square to the wind, a yacht can point upwind, sailing on what is called a close reach. By going first one way and then the other, it can zigzag or "tack" its way into the wind (see *above*).

INTO THE WIND

The crew of a racing yacht rush to trim the sails for the best possible speed when sailing on a close reach (*right*). The person steering the boat works out the best moment to turn or "go about" onto the other tack.

MODEL BOAT
PART 3

PADDLES

1 To add paddles to your model, trace the two paddle parts in the plans (parts **F** and **G**). Cut the two parts from a fruit juice carton, but check they are not as wide as your hull.

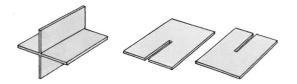

2 Make a slit halfway down each rectangle and slide the two together to form a cross-shaped paddle. Tape two sticks to the sides of the hull so they stick out at least 2 inches beyond the end of the bottle.

3 Tape a rubber band to the paddle end and wrap the ends of the band around the sticks. Then wind up the rubber band and place your boat in a bathtub. Watch as the paddle spins and your boat moves forward.

Racing eights (*right*) have four people rowing on each side, and a cox at the stern to steer. Strength and timing can push an eight through the water at more than 15 miles per hour.

Propellers are sometimes called screws because of the way they cut through water.

ROWING POWER

Oars are like long paddles. They swivel in oarlocks—U-shaped fixtures on the sides of the boat. By dipping them into the water and pulling, the rower makes the boat move. The boat is steered by pulling more on one oar than the other.

Boat moves forward

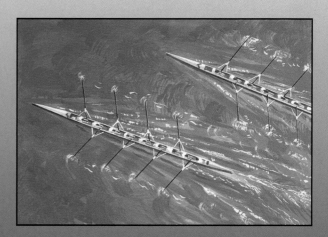

PROPELLER POWER

Propellers have to spin very fast to create any real thrust. But they are underwater all the time, so unlike paddles, no energy is wasted in lifting them out of the water.

As a propeller spins, its curved shape makes water flow faster over the front edge (*top*). This creates an area of low pressure. The higher pressure at the back pushes the boat forward.

PADDLE POWER

Rotating paddles work like waterwheels, pushing the water backward and driving the ship forward (*right*). However, big waves can easily damage paddle wheels, so they are more suited to rivers.

Oar pushes the water back

PADDLES

Boats can also be driven through the water by pushing it backward. Oars work because they act like levers, increasing the force of the rower's efforts in the water. Paddles also push water back, but propellers use differences in water pressure to make a ship move forward.

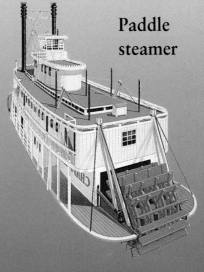

Paddle steamer

MODEL BOAT
PART 4

PROPELLERS

1 To make a propeller, cut out part **H** from a piece of plastic (like a detergent bottle). Then make a small hole in the middle (*right*).

2 Push a rubber band through an empty ballpoint pen tube. Then push a toothpick through the loop at one end. Hook a piece of flexible wire through the other end (*right*).

3 Push the ends of the wire through the hole in the propeller. Wind them around tightly (*above left*).

4 Hold the ends of the propeller (*below*). Twist the right side toward you and the left side away from you. This curved shape is important.

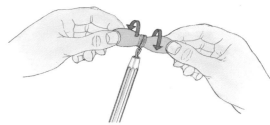

5 Tape the pen to the bottom of the hull, and wrap two rubber bands around both if extra support is needed (*below*). Then wind the propeller around and around. Place the bottle in the bathtub, and let go. Watch the spinning propeller drive the boat forward.

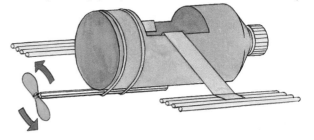

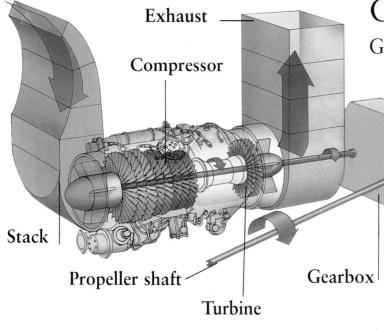

Exhaust

Compressor

Stack

Propeller shaft

Turbine

Gearbox

GAS TURBINES

Gas turbines in modern ships are like jet engines (*left*). They suck in air through a stack, compress (squeeze) it, mix it with fuel, and burn the mixture.

The exploding mix spins the blades of the fan-shaped turbine, which is linked by a shaft to a gearbox.

On diesel electric ships, the gas turbine turns a generator that produces electricity for a motor. This motor then drives the propeller.

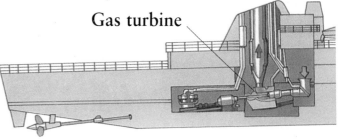

Gas turbine

A small nuclear reactor is used to boil water, produce steam, and drive the turbines in nuclear-powered submarines.

NUCLEAR POWER

Nuclear submarines can stay submerged for months. The nuclear reactor needs no air and can run for years without refuelling. To be as quiet as possible, submarine propellers spin slowly. To create enough thrust, they are larger and have more blades.

Ship's propeller

Submarine propeller

THE POWER SUPPLY

Modern ships are driven by internal combustion engines—diesel engines for cargo ships, gasoline engines for smaller boats, and gas turbines for warships. The age of steam at sea is over, except for nuclear ships which use steam turbines.

Hovercraft are driven by aircraft propellers that can be swiveled to change direction.

JETSKIS

In jetskis the propeller is powered by a motorcycle engine and enclosed in a tube. Water enters the tube at the front and is accelerated by the propeller, coming out as a jet at the back (*above*).

Jetski project

Turn your hull into a jetski by cutting a larger hole in the top, and a small round hole at the back. Place a balloon in the bottle, with the end sticking out of the hole at the back. Blow up the balloon, and still holding the end, place the boat in the bathtub. Let go, and the air rushing out of the back drives the bottle forward.

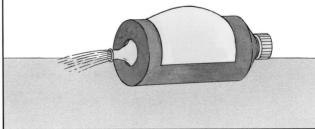

CONTROLS

Ships move slowly compared to trains or planes, but they need good controls. Most steer using a rudder at the stern. This is usually a flat piece of metal that swings like a door. Some naval vessels turn very fast by having two propellers—one is reversed while the other goes full ahead. Many ships also have controls to stop them from rolling too much.

Attaching a rudder to your boat

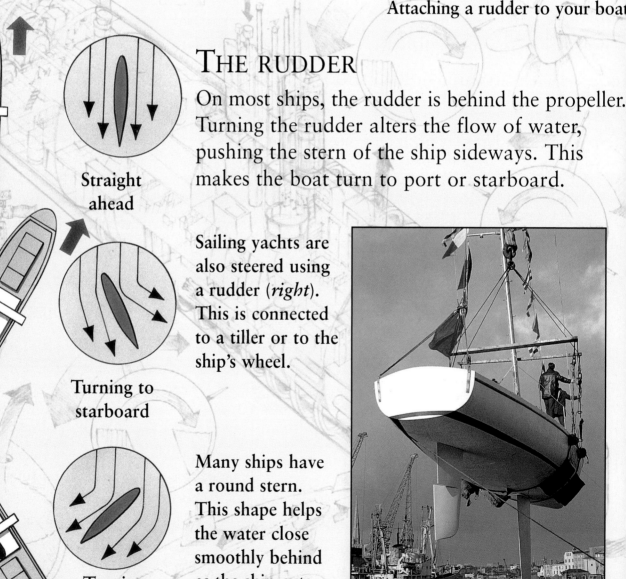

Straight ahead

Turning to starboard

Turning to port

THE RUDDER

On most ships, the rudder is behind the propeller. Turning the rudder alters the flow of water, pushing the stern of the ship sideways. This makes the boat turn to port or starboard.

Sailing yachts are also steered using a rudder (*right*). This is connected to a tiller or to the ship's wheel.

Many ships have a round stern. This shape helps the water close smoothly behind as the ship cuts through the water.

Hydroplane

SUBMARINES

A submarine flows through the water like an airship through the air. By tilting large panels at the stern and bow, called hydroplanes, the submarine's pilot can control the stream of water flowing past.

STABILIZERS

Stabilizers reduce rolling in rough seas. They are used to make passenger ships more comfortable, and to prevent cargo from moving.

Altering the angle of the stabilizer raises or lowers that side of the ship (*left*).

The bow and stern hydroplanes work together to steer a submarine left and right and up and down. Look at the diagram *below* to see how this works.

MODEL BOAT
PART 5

RUDDER

1 To make a rudder, bend a piece of wire to form a right angle, making the handle of your rudder. Then cut out part I from a fruit juice carton. Slide the wire through a straw and attach the square to the bottom of the wire. Then tape the straw to the back of your paddleboat (see page 70).

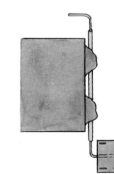

2 Wind up the paddle and place the boat in a bathtub. As the boat moves forward, turn the handle of the rudder from one side to the other and see what this does to your boat's course.

THE VOYAGE

A ship's controls are most important in shipping lanes or when coming into port—stopping a big oil tanker can take several miles. Modern sea lanes are very busy, and some cargos (like oil) can be heavy and dangerous. Luckily, today's pilots have many hi-tech instruments to warn them about possible problems.

A ship's speed is still measured in knots (1 knot = 1.15 mph), from when sailors used ropes with evenly spaced knots to measure their speed.

NAVIGATION

Early navigators followed the sun and the stars. They used simple instruments like the astrolabe (*right*) and compass—and a lot of guesswork!

Fortunately, accurate charts, radio, radar, and navigation satellites have come to the aid of modern sailors.

Astrolabe

SHIP

Sonar depth finder

Radar reflector on buoy

Lighthouses still highlight dangerous spots on the coast. The safest routes through shallow waters are marked by buoys (*right*) in different colors. Some buoys also have radar reflectors.

DOCKING

Large cargo ships need the help of tugs and pilot boats to dock safely at many ports. Some load and unload at offshore mooring buoys. Ferries use thrusters—small propellers at the bow and stern—to turn in tight spaces (*right*).

In port, the use of containers speeds up loading and unloading.

Satellites in orbit around the Earth can now give a precise position for any ship equipped with a GPS (Global Positioning System) receiver. The receivers measure how long signals take to reach them from several satellites at the same time.

Signal from satellite

Lighthouse

Radar signal from shore

The bridge of a modern ship (*above*) has accurate navigation equipment for steering the vessel and keeping it safely on course. This includes an automatic pilot (1), electronic navigation (2), radar (3), and compass (4).

RADAR

Radar has made the job of avoiding collision in busy shipping lanes easier—though a good lookout is still needed. Radar works by sending out bursts of radio waves. These reflect off metal objects such as other ships. The returning signals are picked up by a receiver that shows other ships as glowing green dots on a screen.

SONAR

Ships use sonar systems—bouncing sound signals off the bottom—to make sure the water is deep enough. Submarines use the same device to detect underwater objects.

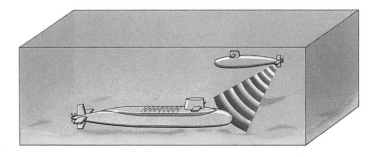

A

B

C

O
H

F

G

74

PLANS FOR MODEL SHIP

A modern jet has a lot of controls to insure safety.

CHAPTER 4—AIRCRAFT

THE SCIENCE OF FLYING

Two things must happen if a plane is going to fly. First, the lift from its wings must be greater than its weight. Second, it needs to travel fast enough for its wings to work. To do this, the thrust of its engines must be bigger than the drag of the air that holds it back.

LIFT

Air flowing over the wings lifts a plane upward. Wings work because of their airfoil shape—a rounded top and a flatter bottom surface.

DRAG

DRAG

When you cycle fast, you can feel the force of the air pushing against you and slowing you down. This is known as drag. How much drag a plane creates depends on its shape and smoothness.

Wings create drag as well as lift, and the faster the plane goes, the more drag it creates.

Wright Flyer I

Most planes have a tail plane at the back. But the Wright Brothers' Flyer 1, the first powered plane, had a tail plane in front.

Boeing 727

ALL CHANGE

The forces on a plane change all the time. For example, fuel makes a big difference to a plane's weight. As it gets used up, the plane becomes lighter. Voyager, the first plane to fly around the world non-stop, weighed almost four times as much when its fuel tanks were full.

THRUST

Both propellers and jets work by driving a large amount of air backward, which has the effect of pushing the plane forward.

Voyager

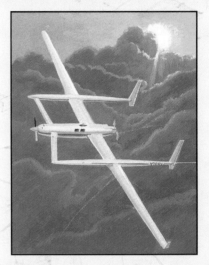

IFT

THRUST

WEIGHT

WEIGHT

Gravity pulls the weight of the plane, its passengers (*left*), luggage, and fuel downward. The more the weight, the greater the thrust needed from the engines. To minimize the weight, planes are made from light materials that are very strong.

To make your glider you will need: paper, thin cardboard, scissors, tape, craft glue, pencil, ruler, and modeling clay. For other projects you will need: thick cardboard, rubber bands, matchsticks, hairdryer, straws, bendy wire, two jar lids, a stick, ballpoint pen, and a candle.

Model glider project box

Science experiment project box

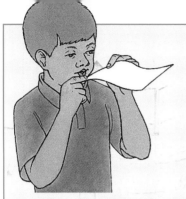

WINGS

Wings create lift in two ways: by their airfoil shape, and by the angle at which they are set. Air rushing past the wing creates the lift. But the flow of air must be smooth.

Increasing the angle of the wing increases lift, but only up to a point. Too great an angle causes turbulence, making the wing "stall" and lose lift.

A piece of paper can work like a wing. Hold it in front of your mouth and blow across the top surface. This lifts the paper upward, because the air on top is moving faster.

1. Wings move through the air.

3. Low pressure caused by the faster flow above the wing creates lift.

AIRFOILS

Most wings are airfoils. This means that they have a rounded upper surface and a flatter bottom surface. This special shape works like this:

1. As the plane moves forward, the air flows both under and over it.
2. Air flowing over the wing moves faster than that below it.
3. This creates an area of low pressure above the wing, sucking it upward.

4. The lift created overcomes the force of gravity pulling downward.

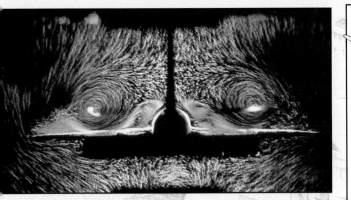

WIND TEST

Wind tunnels are used to test how air flows over a wing. The Concorde's unusual wings produce vortices—little whirlpools of air near the tips for extra lift at low speeds.

2. The shape of the wing forces air flowing over it to go faster than the air flowing below.

FEEL THE FORCE

Test your model wing by pulling it through the air. You will feel it rising in your hand as the air rushes over it. Then alter the angle of the wing. Does this affect the amount of lift it produces?

MODEL GLIDER
PART 1

WINGS

1 It's time to put the science into action. On pages 94-95 are plans to build your glider. Just photocopy or transfer them onto paper and cut the shapes out. Ask an adult to help as careful cutting will make your glider fly better. To start, cut out wing shape **A**, and score along the dotted lines.

2 Carefully fold the edge of piece **A** into an L-shape (*above*). Glue this L-shape down, and pull it slightly toward the opposite edge. This makes the curved airfoil shape that gives your glider lift (*right*).

3 Cut out wing part **B** and fold it along the dotted line. Then glue it to **A**, next to the part that has been folded over (*above*). Make sure the ends of **A** and **B** line up correctly.

4 To make the other wing, cut out parts **A** and **B** and turn them over. Fold along the dotted lines in the opposite direction, and glue as you did on the first wing. Check that you have made both left and right wings.

THE BODY

Early planes were made of wood, held together by wire, an
covered in a fabric skin that added little to their strength
(*right*). They often had two or more short wings on each
side, because these materials couldn't make a long wing
strong enough. A big change came when the plane's skin
became part of the structure and metal was used instead of
wood. The skin fitted over a framework of ribs and frames.

Strength

1 A sheet of thin
cardboard seems
to have little strength. If you
roll it into a tube around two
jar lids, it is still easily bent
(*below*). But glue rings of thick
cardboard to it, and it has
strength in one direction.

2 Glue strips of cardboard
to the tube for strength in the
other direction (*below*). It is
now much more difficult to
bend or crush, even though it
is made of cardboard. This is
how a plane's fuselage is
built. Since it is made from
metal, it is incredibly strong.

Rib

Frame   Skin

**B-17 Flying
Fortress**

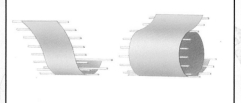

METAL SKIN

The B-17 Flying Fortress (*main
picture*) used aluminum alloys
for ribs, frames, and skin in the
1940s. Today, most planes are
made in a similar way.

Sikorsky Le Grand

UNDER PRESSURE

Have you been on a carnival ride and felt the pressure on your body as you spin around? These centrifugal forces act on a plane every time it turns in the air. This is why a plane needs to be strong as well as light.

The ribs in the fuselage (body) and the struts in the wings have circles cut out of them to make them lighter.

MODEL GLIDER
PART 2
FUSELAGE

1 Two sections make up the fuselage of your glider—parts **C** and **D**. Like a real plane, they are strengthened by frames—**E**, **F**, and **G**. To make **C**, roll it into a tube, then glue it.

2 Make part **D** the same way. Then cut out **E**, **F**, and **G** from cardboard. Push frame **E** down into **C** using a straw, until it is wedged in. Then glue **F** and **G** just inside the openings of **C** and **D**. This should leave an overlap so that **C** slips over **D**. Glue parts **C** and **D** together.

tail flaps

3 After this, fold **H** along the dotted lines as shown (*below*). Then glue **H** over the join between **C** and **D**. But make sure **H** lines up with the tail flaps on top of **C**.

4 You have now made the main body and the wings. Turn to page 86 to join them together.

ENGINES

Wings need air rushing past them to create lift. So planes need to be driven forward by pushing lots of air back. Both propellers and jet engines use angled spinning blades that cut through the air and push it backward. Propeller planes use less fuel but fly more slowly. Jets are more powerful, with greater speed and range.

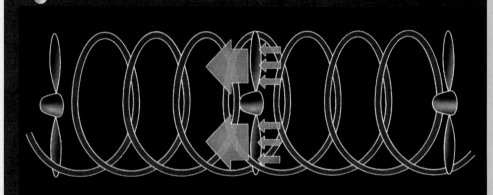

As the propeller spins, the air pressure in front of it drops. The high pressure behind pushes the plane forward. The blades are curved to act like screws being driven through the air.

PROPELLERS

Propeller blades are shaped like wings, with an airfoil section. They are made from aluminum, carbon fiber, and plastic.

Two, three, or four blades make up each propeller. On most planes, the angle (or pitch) of each blade can be changed to produce the best performance for climbing or cruising.

High pitch creates little drag and is used for cruising.

Low pitch creates thrust at takeoff.

The Dornier Do X, the biggest plane of its time, had twelve piston engines—six pulling, six pushing. Even so, they only just gave it enough power to take off.

Pushing air

Cut a propeller shape out of cardboard, twisting it at both ends to make an airfoil shape. Then wrap a piece of bendy wire around the middle. Attach this to a rubber band, and pull it through an empty pen case. Then slip a matchstick over the end. Holding the match with one hand, twist the propeller around and around. Then let go and feel it blow your face (*left*).

JET ENGINES

Jet engines suck in air at one end and force it out of the other at very high speed. They work by mixing fuel with air and burning it. As it burns, the mix expands and pours out of the back of the engine. The gases that rush backward thrust the plane in the opposite direction—forward.

A TURBOJET ENGINE

1. Air is sucked into the front of the engine by a spinning fan called a compressor.

2. The space narrows as the air flows into the engine, squeezing it and making it hotter.

REACTION

Engine moves forward

ACTION

Gases thrust to rear

3. As air enters the combustion chamber, nozzles spray in fuel, which is ignited (set alight).

4. The burning mixture expands, and hot gases roar out the back, creating thrust.

The big squeeze

1. Modern jet engines use the simple principle of compressing (squeezing) air. The air is taken in through a large opening. This narrows, making the air speed up.
2. Try this using a hairdryer set to cold—but ask an adult to help. Can it blow out a candle 5 feet away? The air spreads out so it probably can't.
3. But if you put a cardboard funnel shape over the dryer, the faster stream should blow out the candle.

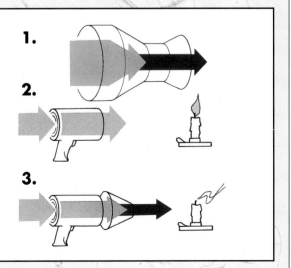

THE PISTON ENGINE

A piston engine works by sucking fuel and air into the cylinder. It then sets it alight with an electric spark. The explosion forces the piston down. The piston is connected to a shaft that drives the propeller. Several cylinders often work together, firing one after the other to spin the propeller around.

In this six-cylinder engine (*above*), the pistons are laid flat. But in older planes they were often arranged in a circle (rotary), *below*.

Trilander

Propellers are widely used on smaller aircraft that need to save fuel rather than fly fast (*left*).

PROPELLER PLANES

Propellers are used by light planes or short-distance passenger planes. Helicopters use propellers in the form of rotors. Both are driven either by four-stroke multi-cylindered piston engines or more commonly by turbojets.

A tail rotor stops a helicopter from spinning around

ROTORS AND PROPELLERS

The V-22 Osprey tries to combine the advantages of an airplane and a helicopter. It has engines that rotate so that it can take off vertically, using its propellers like a helicopter's rotors. Then it swings its engines 90 degrees to turn into an airplane.

TWISTING ROTORS

Rotor blades are controlled by a swashplate. Tilting the swashplate changes the angle of the rotors. This makes the helicopter go up or down, forward or back (*right*).

Swashplate

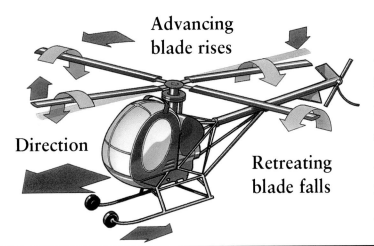

Advancing blade rises

Direction

Retreating blade falls

As each rotor blade travels toward the front of the helicopter, the air flowing over it increases (*left*). This creates lift, and the blade tip rises. As it travels to the back, the tip falls. This makes the blades flap up and down as they spin around.

Gearbox

Main rotor

Turbojet

HELICOPTER ENGINES

Modern helicopters use turbojets to drive the main rotor and the tail rotor. The turbojet engines suck air in. They squeeze it, mix it with fuel, then set it alight. The hot gases spin a turbine (fan), which is linked to both rotors by a gearbox.

Shaft connects engine to tail rotor

AUTOGYRO

The autogyro uses a free-spinning rotor as a wing. As the autogyro propeller drives it forward, the rotor spins to create lift. The autogyro cannot hover like a helicopter.

Autogyro

CONTROLS

To fly planes safely, pilots must be able to control the air flowing over the wings and the tail. To do so, they use hinged flaps—ailerons on the trailing edge of wings, elevators on the tail, and a rudder on the fin. These redirect the flow of air to create forces that make the plane go where the pilot wants. For example, the plane is turned by rolling it with the ailerons at the same time as turning with the rudder.

Adjusting your glider's ailerons

MODEL GLIDER
PART 3
ADDING THE WINGS

1 Add the wings to the body. Glue the tabs on the end of each wing to the top of the fuselage above section **H**.

2 Glue part **I** under both wings.

Slots

Spoilers

Aileron

Flaps

YAW
The rudder controls the direction the plane is pointing, called yaw. It helps the plane stay on course in windy conditions.

ROLL
Ailerons roll the plane from side to side. Some aerobatic planes can complete a roll, all the way around, in a single second.

PITCH
Pitch is the angle at which the plane points above or below the horizon. The pilot controls it using the elevators on the tail.

FLYING YOUR GLIDER

The basic control surfaces are the same with your glider. The rudder and tail are so sensitive you can just bend them to control pitch and yaw. To control roll, cut ailerons into the wings and fold along the dotted lines. See how your glider changes direction when you move the control surfaces.

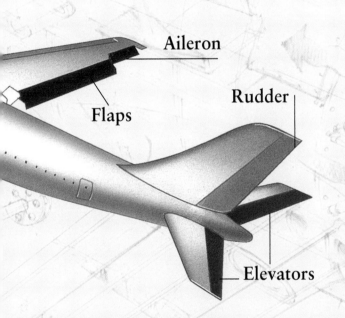

Aileron

Flaps

Rudder

Elevators

EXTRA CONTROLS

Airliners also have big flaps to extend the wing and increase lift. Slots are the movable leading edges on the wing. They increase lift at slow speeds.

Spoilers are flaps that appear just after touchdown. They produce a downforce so the tires carry the weight of the plane, and the brakes work effectively.

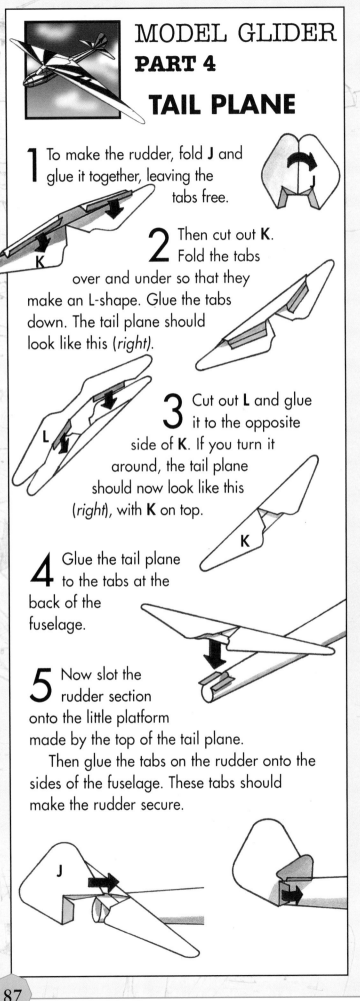

MODEL GLIDER
PART 4
TAIL PLANE

1 To make the rudder, fold **J** and glue it together, leaving the tabs free.

2 Then cut out **K**. Fold the tabs over and under so that they make an L-shape. Glue the tabs down. The tail plane should look like this (*right*).

3 Cut out **L** and glue it to the opposite side of **K**. If you turn it around, the tail plane should now look like this (*right*), with **K** on top.

4 Glue the tail plane to the tabs at the back of the fuselage.

5 Now slot the rudder section onto the little platform made by the top of the tail plane.
Then glue the tabs on the rudder onto the sides of the fuselage. These tabs should make the rudder secure.

CONTROL SYSTEMS

Many planes are still controlled by a system of powered cables that link the control surfaces to the pilot's controls.

But in newer airplanes, the control stick (*right*) feeds the pilot's commands to computers that not only check the commands but makes sure they are safe. Signals are sent along wires to motors that move the control surfaces. This is called "fly-by-wire."

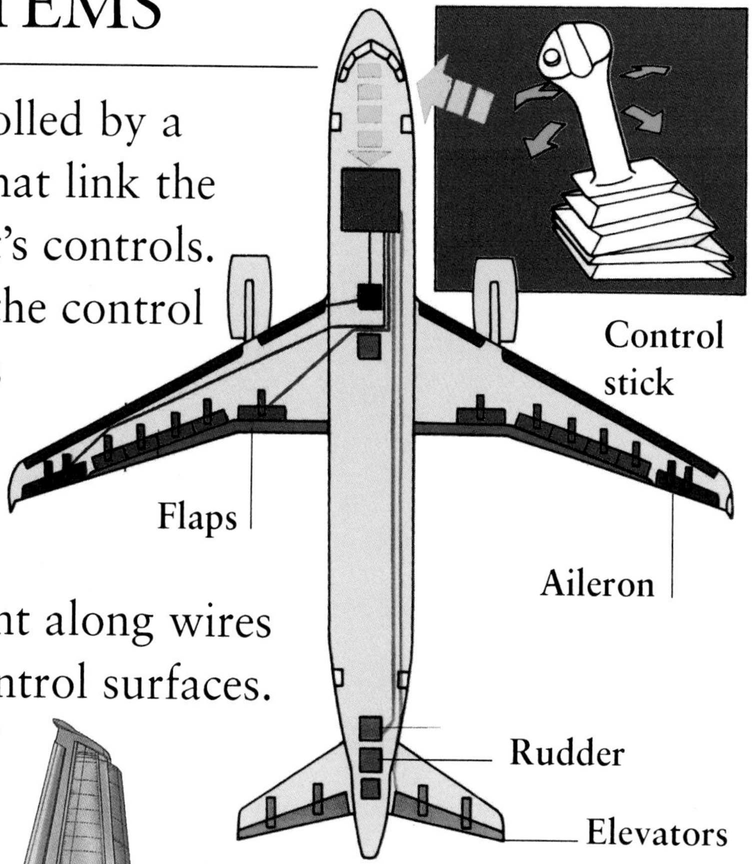

Control stick

Flaps

Aileron

Rudder

Elevators

BETTER ENGINES

Modern jet engines are bigger and more reliable. Big airliners with two instead of four engines are now common.

SAFETY CONTROLS

A system of computers checks and rechecks the aircraft's systems at all times. If one computer fails, another takes over. These include fire detectors and extinguishers, fuel, hydraulic, navigation, and electric systems.

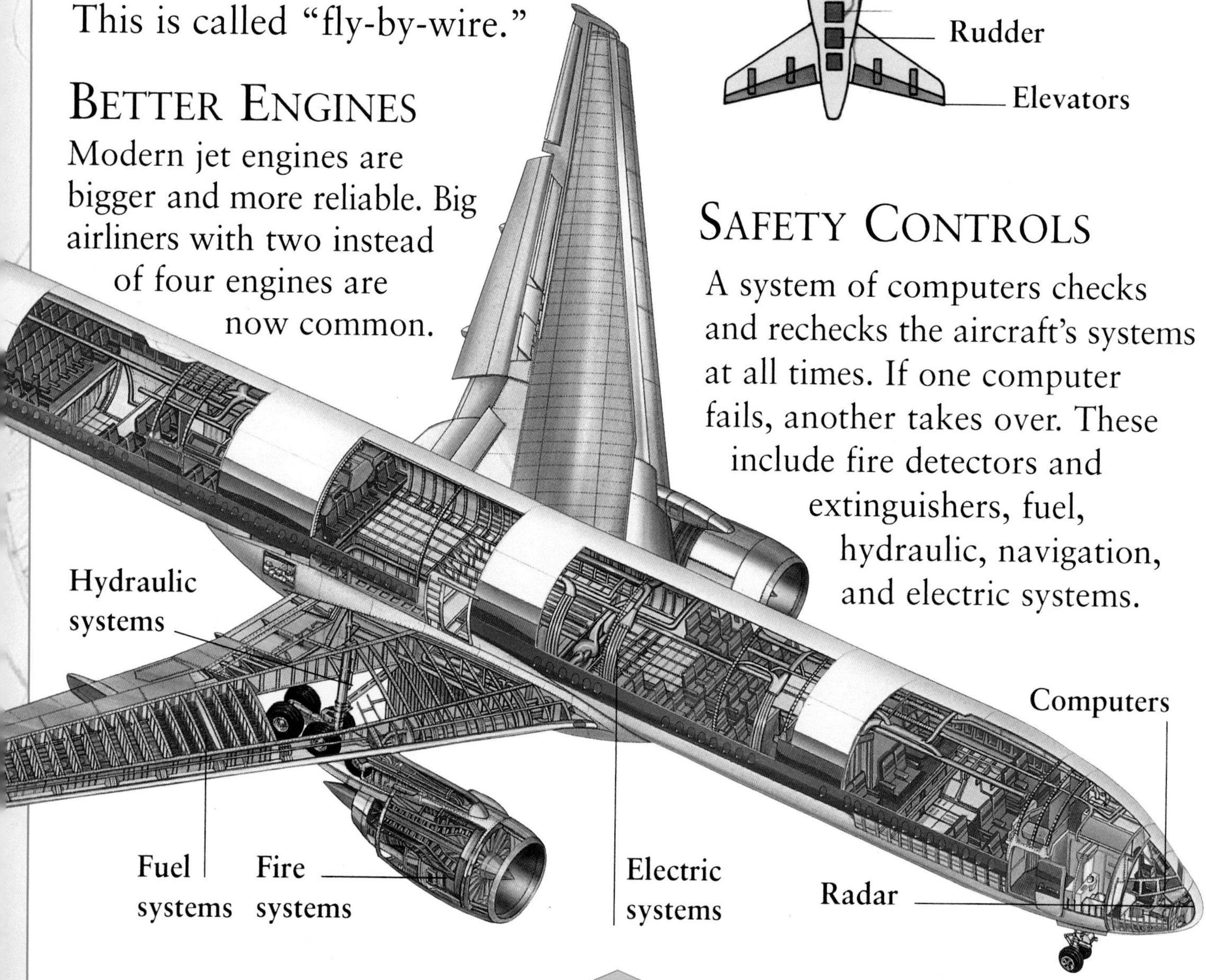

Hydraulic systems

Computers

Fuel systems

Fire systems

Electric systems

Radar

AIRBUS COCKPIT
Here are the main
cockpit controls:

1 Ignition
2 Radar
3 EADI (page 92)
4 Control stick
5 Thrust levers

The autopilot is used
for most of the flight,
although one pilot is
always keeping an eye
on the control panels.

NERVE CENTER

At the front of most planes is the cockpit,
or flight deck. The first pilot (captain)
and second pilot sit in the two front
seats. They share the basic flying and
navigating roles. Electronic equipment
monitors the engines. A special
computer, the autopilot, can fly the
plane on its own.

TAIL FLYING

YF-22

The YF-22 is an
advanced fighter
aircraft with a very
sophisticated fly-by-wire
control system. This allows
the pilot to attempt things that
are impossible on other planes,
such as flying the plane "on its tail."

Early flyers such as the Wright
brothers controlled their
planes by twisting
the wings with
wires (*right*).
  This method
may be used in
  future planes in place of ailerons,
flaps, and elevators, using electronic
fly-by-wire controls (*above*).

89

TAKEOFF

Takeoff and landing are the busiest periods for the flight crew. Today's airports are very busy, so the pilot needs to be able to take off and land safely in a very short space of time. As the plane taxies out to the runway, the pilot always gives the ailerons, elevators, and rudder a final check.

You may need to add some modeling clay to the nose of your plane to balance it.

MAXIMUM LIFT

The engines are always operated at full power on takeoff, though this can be very noisy. The wing flaps are fully extended to increase the size of the wing. This gives the maximum possible lift at a time when the aircraft is heaviest, with a full load of fuel.

Flow of air while the plane speeds up

Flow of air at takeoff

GAINING SPEED
When the wings are angled slightly, they don't create much lift. But they don't produce much drag either. This helps the airliner to speed up on takeoff.

TAKEOFF
When the plane is traveling fast enough to take off, the nose of the aircraft is pulled up. This sudden change in the angle of the wings creates a lot of lift.

MODEL GLIDER
PART 5

COCKPIT & NOSE

Here are the final two sections for building the glider—adding the cockpit section and the nose. If you want to paint your glider, use paints that aren't water-based (the water will crinkle the paper).

2 To make the nose section, glue the two ends of **O** together, then the two ends of **P**. Slot **P** over **O** and glue inside using the tabs. Glue **Q** to **P**. But don't glue the nose on until you have tested for balance (page 90).

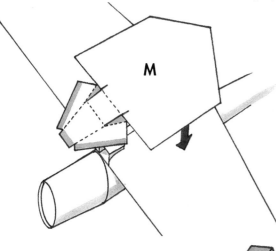

1 Cut out section **M**, the cockpit. Bend the sides under the top and glue it down onto the top of the wings. This section also strengthens the join between the wings and the body.

3 Finally, fold **R** into an accordion shape and glue the folds together. Cut the edges off with scissors to make a round shape, and glue **R** to the body where **C** meets **D**. Go back to page 87 for flying tips.

STALLING

However, if the nose is pulled up too much, a stall can occur. Air stops flowing across the upper surface so the wings stop producing lift. Air flowing under the wing creates more drag. A plane can drop out of the sky if it stalls.

Stalling—when air flowing over the top surface of the wing breaks away.

LANDING AT SEA

To land on water, some aircraft have floats instead of wheels, or bodies shaped like boats. To land on an aircraft carrier, aircraft have a special hook that is caught by ropes stretched across the deck.

A Chinook helicopter drops its load before landing.

THE LANDING

When landing, the autopilot picks up two sets of beams, which guide the plane in. At about 60 feet from the ground, the pilot brings the plane's nose up to slow it down. Once the plane touches down, the pilot uses brakes, spoilers, and reverse thrust to bring it to a halt.

Even on automatic pilot, the crew watch their instruments carefully. An altimeter shows height, the ASI (air speed indicator) shows speed, a compass shows direction, and the EADI (electronic attitude director indicator) shows if the plane is level.

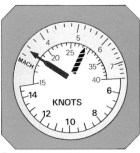

ASI

Compass

EADI

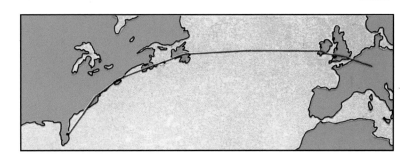

Long flight paths take into account the round shape of the world and air currents such as the jet stream. These high-altitude winds can make a journey much faster in one direction.

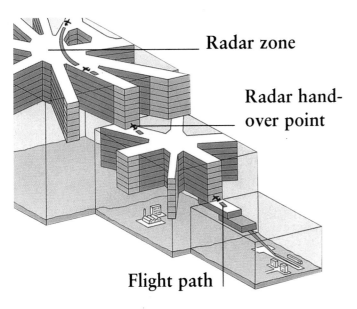

Radar zone

Radar hand-over point

Flight path

STACKING PLANES

If an airliner cannot come straight in for a landing, it is diverted into a stack a few miles from the airport. Here, waiting aircraft circle at different levels, slowly flying down as earlier aircraft are called to break off and approach the runway. In busy airports, a plane will take off or land every minute.

RADAR

Airliners are brought in to land using radar beams to keep them on the right flight path. Air traffic controllers (*right*) bring in the planes one at a time, keeping a safe distance between them. The planes appear on the radar screen as glowing green dots (*above*).

A radar transmitter and receiver spins constantly.

Radar works by sending pulses of radio waves from a transmitter. These waves reflect off large metal objects, such as planes. Some of the waves return back to a dish where a receiver picks them up. As the waves travel at the speed of light, they show the plane's position very accurately.

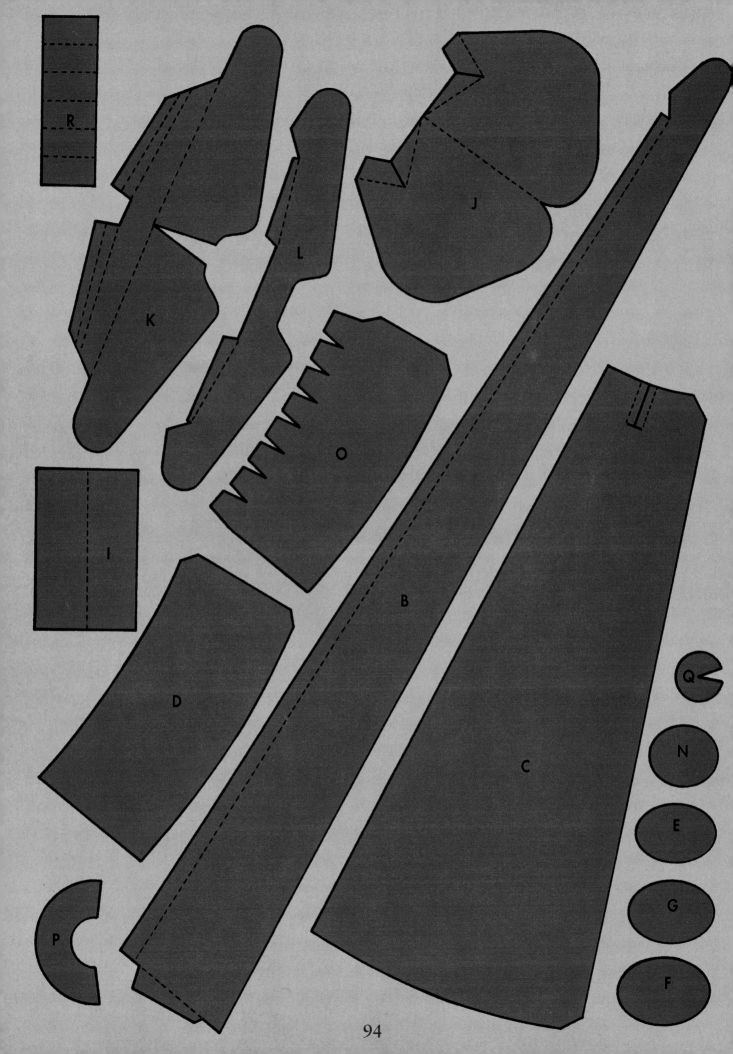

PLANS
FOR
MODEL
GLIDER

CHAPTER 5—TRUCKS, TRACTORS, CRANES

Early machines were powered by humans or animals. The invention of the steam engine allowed machines to produce their own power for the first time.

THE SCIENCE OF MACHINES

The strongest human body can only push or pull an object so much in order to move it around or lift it up against the force of gravity. Machines allow us to push or pull with a bigger force. The first machines changed the forces from our own bodies. Modern machines use forces in the same way but are powered by an engine.

STABILITY

All machines are designed to be stable—they are made so they don't tip over. But this can happen very easily if they are lifting very heavy loads or moving over bumpy ground.

BACKHOE LOADER

A powerful engine creates power for lifting and moving.

DIESEL POWER

Modern machines need to provide power. All modern machines have engines to supply the energy needed, and they usually get their power from large, powerful diesel engines.

Liquid pumped along pipes powers the attachments on machines like this backhoe loader. This way of changing forces is called hydraulics.

CRANES

Cranes are machines that lift loads into the air. Some cranes are mobile, but the biggest ones are attached to the ground. Learn how both types use levers and pulleys.

Mobile crane

The cab provides a safe place for the operator to control the machine.

Different attachments mean that one vehicle can apply forces in different ways to suit any job.

Wide, chunky tires spread out the force of gravity and give a good grip in muddy conditions.

actor

To make the projects, you will need: thick and thin cardboard, single-sided corrugated cardboard, a craft knife, 3 or 4 pebbles, scissors, craft glue, acrylic paint, 1/4-inch diameter wooden dowel, screw eyelets and hook, string, a thin rubber band about 1/2-inch long, 2 headless matchsticks, a large wooden bead, and 4 empty thread spools.

Model crane project box

Science experiment project box

TRACKS

All mobile machines need to push and pull against the ground to move around. Some use tracks instead of wheels because on uneven ground the wheels might lift off, making the machine unstable. Tracks spread the weight out evenly, and part of the track is always in contact with the ground.

This heavy machine uses tracks to remain stable while working on uneven ground.

No cleats   **Cleats**

Try this—do cleats give a better grip?

Traction

Traction is the scientific word for grip. Playing sports on a muddy field would be dangerous without good grip. The cleats on a soccer shoe help you start, stop, and turn without slipping.

The tracks on this bulldozer grip like cleats.

CAT F R 973

CAT

SNOW PLOW

Snow plows often combine wheels for steering and tracks for grip. Snow can fill the tread on wheels, but it falls off the tracks as they turn.

TRACKS

Tracks are made from many individual links joined together to form a flexible band around two wheels at the front and back of the vehicle. When the wheels turn, the whole track turns and pushes against the ground, giving more grip.

To keep themselves from sinking in soft ground, some machines have lots of wheels and a big tread (*right*). Tread is the spacing of the grooves and ridges on a tire. Each pair of wheels has its own system of springs so that all wheels stay in contact with the ground.

MODEL CRANE
PART 1
WHEEL BASE

1 MAKE THE BASE
To make your model crane, first trace section **A** onto thick cardboard from the plans on pages 118-119. Cut **A** out and fold it along the dotted lines. Then glue the end and side flaps together. When the glue is dry, paint your wheel base.

glue

glue

A

2 ADD THE WHEELS
Collect 4 empty thread spools. You will need 2 pieces of wooden dowel or 2 pencils 8 inches long. Fit each dowel into a thread spool, then push the dowel through the axle holes. Then attach another spool to the other end.

A

3 MAKE THE TRACKS
Cut out the tracks from single-sided corrugated cardboard, and glue **C** and **D** to the smooth side of **B**.

10 in.

B
2 in.

C
D
1/4 in.

10 in.

C B

D

4 ATTACH THE TRACKS
Now paint the tracks. When they are dry, wrap them around the wheels and glue the ends together.

STABILITY

Machines need to be both balanced and stable. Balanced means that they do not fall over on their own. Stable means that if they do lean over, they fall back to their original position.

An object is balanced if the center of gravity (the average position of the weight) is between the wheels. It is stable until the center of gravity moves outside the wheels. Keeping the weight near the ground makes things more stable.

A dump truck is well balanced when the dumper is down. As it lifts up, its load moves toward the back. If the truck is stable, its front wheels will not lift off the ground.

Weight of load

Adding weight to the base of your model will make it more stable.

ON A SLOPE

Tractors and diggers often have to drive across sloping ground. Early tractors tipped over if the slope was too great. Modern tractors are built with the weight kept low to make them more stable.

STABLE CRANES

Cranes need to be able to hold heavy loads (A) away from their base. To keep them from falling over, a counterweight (B) is held on the opposite side to make sure the center of gravity remains over the base.

Weight of engine balances weight of load as it is tipped.

If center of gravity is between wheels, truck stays stable.

MODEL CRANE
PART 2

THE BODY

1 MAKE THE BODY
Trace part **E** from the plans and cut from thick cardboard. Then fold in the sides and glue them together. Don't forget to cut out holes **E1**, **E2**, **E3**, **E4**, and **E5**!

E5   E
E4
E2
E1   E3

2 MAKE TOP PIVOT
Cut out part **F** from thick cardboard and gently roll it over a large cardboard tube or a rolling pin. Then glue its ends together.

F

3 ATTACH TOP PIVOT
Glue part **F** to the underside of part **E**, making sure that hole **E5** lines up with the center of **F**.

F
E5
E

4 MAKE IT STABLE
Glue 3 or 4 medium-sized pebbles inside the back of base **E**. These make it more stable.

5 ADD STABILITY
Cut out part **G** (the cab) from thick cardboard, fold in the top and sides, and glue them together. Once the glue is dry, glue **G** to **E**.

G
G
E

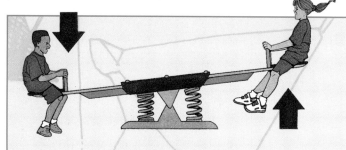

A seesaw is an example of a first-class lever. A smaller person sitting farther away from the fulcrum can balance a heavier person nearer the fulcrum.

LEVERS AND PULLEYS

Levers and pulleys are two of the simplest parts of any machine and can be thought of as simple machines in their own right. They allow us to change the size and direction of forces to match a load. Although the size of the force can be changed, the total energy supplied always remains the same.

A crowbar is also a simple lever. By moving our lever (the crowbar) a long way, we can move a heavy object (the rock) a short distance.

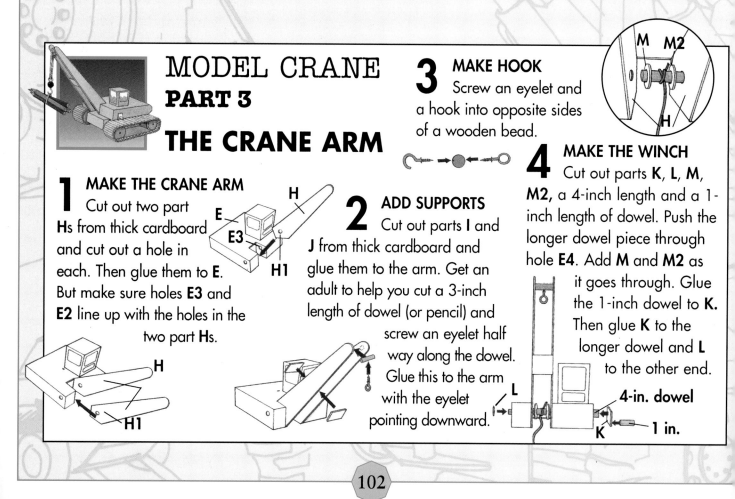

MODEL CRANE
PART 3
THE CRANE ARM

1 MAKE THE CRANE ARM
Cut out two part **H**s from thick cardboard and cut out a hole in each. Then glue them to **E**. But make sure holes **E3** and **E2** line up with the holes in the two part **H**s.

2 ADD SUPPORTS
Cut out parts **I** and **J** from thick cardboard and glue them to the arm. Get an adult to help you cut a 3-inch length of dowel (or pencil) and screw an eyelet half way along the dowel. Glue this to the arm with the eyelet pointing downward.

3 MAKE HOOK
Screw an eyelet and a hook into opposite sides of a wooden bead.

4 MAKE THE WINCH
Cut out parts **K, L, M, M2**, a 4-inch length and a 1-inch length of dowel. Push the longer dowel piece through hole **E4**. Add **M** and **M2** as it goes through. Glue the 1-inch dowel to **K**. Then glue **K** to the longer dowel and **L** to the other end.

4-in. dowel

1 in.

This crane (*left*) uses a pulley (top) to lift its load and a lever (bottom) to move the pulley to the correct position.

HOW LEVERS WORK

Levers are used with forces that turn around the fulcrum, a point where the lever pivots or turns. If we use a longer lever, the force applied to the load increases, but we need to move the lever a greater distance to lift the load by the same amount.

HOW PULLEYS WORK

A simple pulley allows us to change the direction of the force that we apply (the effort). This allows the person or machine doing the pulling to remain on the ground. Compound pulleys increase the size of the force, allowing us to lift much heavier loads.

Effort

COMPOUND PULLEY

Effort

SIMPLE PULLEY

Load   Load

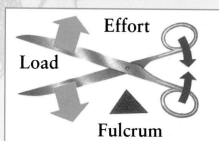

Effort

Load

Fulcrum

A pair of scissors combines two second-class levers. Depending upon where the object to be cut is held, the force is increased or reduced.

COMBINING LEVERS

In machines such as excavators, several levers are often used together. This is called a compound lever. Because the levers do not bend, they swivel at a number of different points. They allow a digger to apply the force where it is needed and to make the force bigger or smaller to match the job.

BOOM

Load

Fulcrum

CLASSES OF LEVERS

There are three classes or types of lever depending upon which side of the fulcrum the effort and load are.

1ST CLASS

Load

Fulcrum

Effort

2ND CLASS

Fulcrum

Effort

Load

3RD CLASS

Load

Fulcrum

Effort

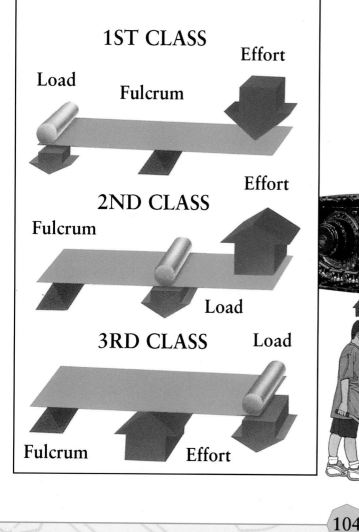

Effort

A wheelbarrow is an example of a second-class lever. The load is close to the fulcrum so the effort needs to travel a long way to lift the load a short distance.

Load

Fulcrum

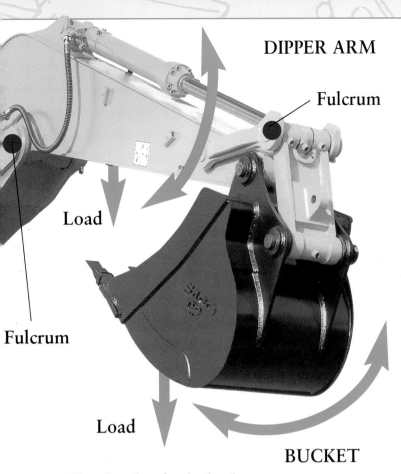

DIPPER ARM

Fulcrum

Load

Fulcrum

Load

BUCKET

The depth of a hole the excavator can dig depends on the length of its dipper arm and boom. This excavator can dig a hole 20 feet deep.

EXCAVATOR

An excavator is a complex machine that combines three levers— the boom, the dipper arm, and the bucket.

The boom is a third-class lever that raises or lowers the dipper. The dipper is a first-class lever that moves the bucket in and out. The bucket is itself another first-class lever that tilts to dig a hole and empty its load.

RAMPS

A ramp is another example of a simple machine. A wedge is another name for a ramp.

We use ramps to help us increase the distance over which we move an object in order to lift it against gravity.

The ancient Egyptians used ramps to help lift stones for the pyramids, and you can see ramps on any modern building site.

Ramp

LIVING LEVERS

The skeletons of living creatures contain many levers. The human forearm is one of the few examples of a third-class lever. Here, the large force of the muscle travels a short distance to make the hand move an object over a large distance.

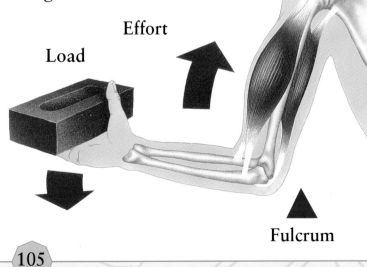

Effort

Load

Fulcrum

DOCKSIDE CRANES

Large cranes, either stationary or on railroad lines, are used to move cargo from ships to trains and trucks for delivery inland.

This crane (*right*) shows the incredible loads that can be carried by compound pulleys.

The control cab for a tower crane is at the top.

The operator has a clear view of the load and construction site, and can move the arm to where it is needed.

CRANES

Cranes are the most common big machines that use pulleys. Because pulleys use cables, they can only pull things upward (unlike levers, which can push *and* pull).

Cranes need to be rigid (stiff) structures that will support the pulley system above the load.

Test out your own pulley system.

Control cab

Concrete counterweights

Pulling power

Make a compound pulley using two coat hangers. Tie the string to the top hanger and then loop it around the bottom hanger. Every loop will increase the mechanical advantage—that is, you can pull a heavier weight by pulling the string farther.

Effort

Load

TOWER CRANE

Tower cranes are used in the construction of modern skyscrapers. At first, the crane does not need to be very tall, but as the building grows so must the crane (see *below*). Normally, the crane stands inside what will become the elevator shaft of the finished building—and the only problem is how to remove the crane once the last story of the building is complete.

The jib, or main arm, of a tower crane is made from steel struts.

The counterweight is used to balance the weight of the jib, which is greater than any load it would need to lift.

Jib

Mobile crane

The load is lifted by a compound pulley system mounted on a trolley. This can be changed for light or heavy loads.

The trolley moves in and out along the jib, and the jib turns to position the load.

Load

MOBILE CRANES

Mobile cranes can be used in more places than tower cranes, but they need special legs to make sure they are stable. The main arm of the crane is often built from a series of levers so that the load can be positioned more accurately.

Tower cranes can build themselves by raising the cab and jib on hydraulic rams and then lifting the next section of tower into place (*right*). Some cranes are over 600 feet tall.

Tower crane

POWER

Building machines and tractors don't move very fast. But they move and lift enormous loads—a big truck can pull up to 600 tons—so they need a very powerful engine.

Nowadays, this is usually a diesel engine and it is often used to provide the power for the hydraulic system (see page 110).

WHAT IS POWER?

Power is the rate of doing work. A task requires the same amount of work whether done quickly or slowly. But greater power is needed to do the work quickly.

For example, a person can supply the energy to move a car (*below*). However, the car will only move slowly, as a person is not very powerful. An engine can supply the same amount of energy in a shorter time.

The Terex Titan (*above*) is the world's largest dump truck. It weighs 603 tons when carrying a full load. It can produce 3,300 horsepower—30 times more than the engine in a small car.

Diesel fuel is cheaper to use than gasoline—especially important in fuel-guzzling monsters like the one above. Big trucks also have up to 20 forward and 4 reverse gears to make the most efficient use of the engine.

HYDRAULIC TRAIN

Sometimes it is more efficient to have only one source of power for all of the motors in a complex machine. Hydraulic trains use a single engine to provide the power to pump a liquid at high pressure to motors attached to each wheel.

ELECTRIC POWER

Tower cranes (*right*) are often powered by electric motors because it's much easier to carry electricity to the top of the crane in wires than to carry diesel in pipes that might leak.

MODEL CRANE
PART 4

ADD THE CABLE

1 SLING YOUR HOOK
Thread string from the winch over the dowel on the crane arm and through the eyelet attached to the bead. Then tie the end to the eyelet that is fixed to the crane arm.

Winch

HYDRAULICS

Hydraulic systems are another way of changing the direction and size of a force. An engine is used to pump a liquid at high pressure down narrow pipes. The liquid pushes against a piston inside a cylinder, forcing it to move.

Hydraulic project

1 Find a thick plastic bag with no holes in it, such as a freezer bag. Seal the end with tape and insert a piece of plastic pipe.

2 Lay the bag on the floor and place a solid board on top. Then fill the pipe with water from a pitcher and connect it to the end of a plastic bottle full of water. All the joints need to be well sealed.

3 Now stand on the board and squeeze the plastic bottle. You will feel yourself being pushed up by the water in the bag!

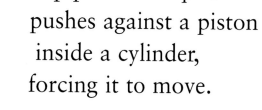

Try this experiment!

Piston rod moves up

Piston rod

1 Liquid pumped into the piston through narrow pipes pushes the piston rod out with a very large force.

2 Another piston is used to rotate the scoop to pick up soil.

MODEL CRANE
PART 5

THE BUCKET ARM

1 MAKE THE ARM

Cut out two part **N**s and parts **P** and **O** from thick cardboard. Glue supports (**P** and **O**) to the two part **N**s. Next, cut a 1-inch length of dowel and screw an eyelet into the dowel. Then glue this dowel to the top of the arms.

2 MAKING THE BUCKET

Cut out two part **Q**s and part **R** from thick cardboard, and part **S** from thin cardboard. Glue the two **Q**s to the edges of part **S**. Once the glue has dried, glue part **R** to the top edge of **S** and **Q**.

3 ATTACH BUCKET TO ARM

Once the glue on the bucket and the arm is dry, glue the base of the arm to the center of **R** and the top of **S**.

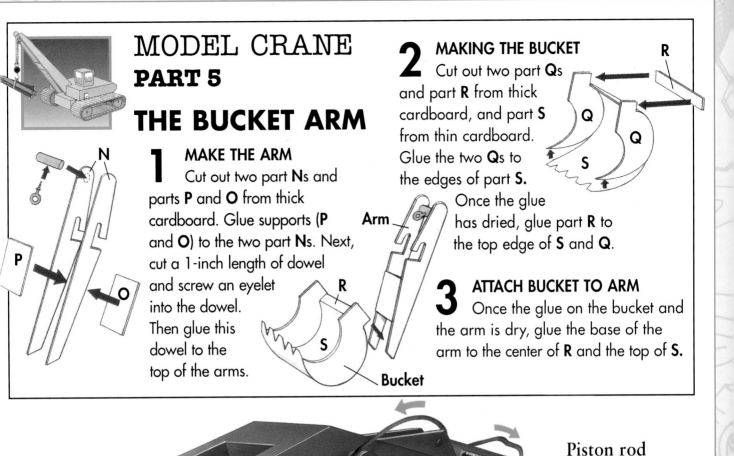

Piston rod moves down

Piston rod

3 Fluid pumped into the top of the cylinder forces the piston down.

4 This raises the arm and the scoop drops its load.

HYDRAULIC ARM

The hydraulic arm uses rigid (stiff) arms that act as levers. They use the force supplied by the hydraulic pistons. In most machines, the pumps that push the hydraulic fluid are driven by the main engine, and all the fluid comes from the same reservoir.

Pressure project

You can create the pressure to pop a cork without using chemicals. Find a plastic drinks bottle at least 1 foot long. Empty the bottle. Place a cork in the top, making sure the bottle is full of air. Now jump on the bottle (see *below*).

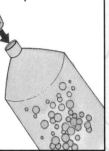

BACKHOE DRILLER

The hydraulic motor of the digger pumps fluid into and out of the piston of the drill in short, sharp bursts.

At the same time, the pistons of the arm press down on the drill to force it into the ground.

CONTROLS

Pneumatics (systems that use compressed air) and hydraulics (systems that use compressed liquids) are both used to control building machines.

Pneumatics are less efficient because the air heats up as it is squashed, but they are simpler because air is simply sucked in from outside.

If you jump on the bottle, the cork shoots out. Your weight squeezes the air inside the bottle, creating pressure on the cork. Be careful!

MODEL CRANE
PART 6

BUCKET ARM

Bucket arm

1 ADD BUCKET ARM
Hook the arm onto the dowel cross bar at the top of the crane arm. Then tie the string from the winch to the eyelet that is connected to the bead and hook.

2 OPERATE BUCKET ARM
Connect the hook on the string to the eyelet on the bucket arm's cross bar. Now you are ready to operate the bucket arm— just turn the winch handle and lift the bucket.

Winch handle

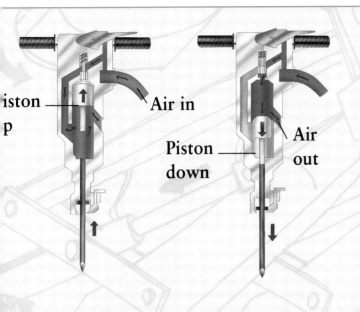

iston
p

Piston
down

Air in

Air
out

PNEUMATIC DRILL

Pneumatic drills use compressed air instead of a fluid to power the drill. Air is pumped from a compressor into the drill. A heavy weight inside the drill is pushed up or down by a series of valves that control the flow of air. The air is then released into the outside world which is why this kind of drill is so noisy.

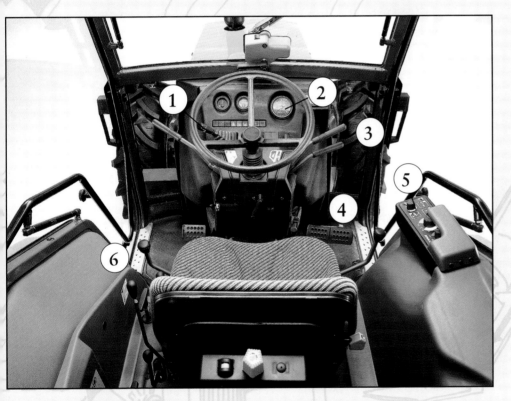

INSIDE THE CAB

1 Lever to select forward or reverse
2 Instrument panel
3 Levers for horn, road and indicator lights
4 Brake and accelerator pedals
5 Starter switch and heating controls
6 Hydraulic control levers

THE CAB

The cab of any vehicle provides protection for the driver and controls to operate the machine. Many controls operate the valves of the hydraulic system. Though there are many systems, the digger only needs one engine.

Power steering (*right*) uses hydraulics to push the wheels to the side. The fluid pumped into the cylinders moves the pistons in and out.

TRUCK SYSTEMS

Trucks carry loads from one place to another. But they still have to do lifting. Every time they travel uphill they lift themselves and their load. The wheels change the turning force of the engine into a force that drives the truck forward. Trucks also use hydraulic systems for dumping their load and for steering.

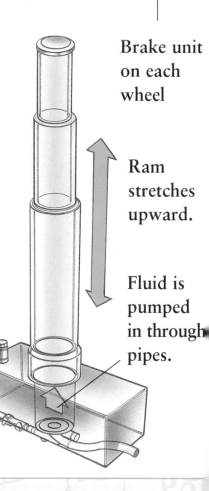

Compressor

Brake unit on each wheel

Ram stretches upward.

Fluid is pumped in through pipes.

Gluing on the track section

Road trucks have a smooth shape to reduce drag.

HYDRAULIC RAMS

Trucks use hydraulic rams to dump their load. A ram works like the pistons in a hydraulic arm, but it stretches like a telescope to many times its length. Several tubes inside each other can be pushed out by hydraulic fluid.

Air is forced between the rim of the wheels and the brake pads. When the air is released, the pads clamp against the wheels.

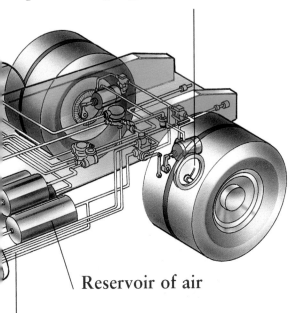

Reservoir of air

Brake lines connect the compressor to the brake units.

AIR BRAKES

Most trucks have air brakes. These use high-pressure air supplied by a compressor. The air pushes in between the inner rim of the wheel and the brake pads or shoes.

When the driver puts his or her foot on the brake, the air is released and the pads spring against the wheels, stopping the truck.

A fork lift truck carries standard loads. Its forks fit underneath a palette or container. Then it uses hydraulic rams to lift and stack the load.

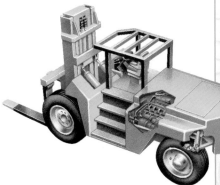

TRUCK CABS

Truck drivers spend long hours on the road, so their cabs are built for comfort.

1 Citizen's Broadcast (CB) radio
2 Instrument panel
3 Folding tables for maps
4 Plenty of storage space
5 Bed

MODEL CRANE
PART 7
ADD THE PIVOT

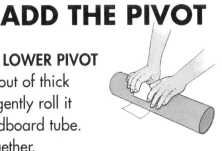

1 MAKE THE LOWER PIVOT
Cut part **T** out of thick cardboard and gently roll it over a large cardboard tube. Glue its ends together.

T

2 ADD PIVOT TO WHEEL BASE
When the glue is dry on the lower pivot, glue **T** onto the dotted circle on the wheel base.

ALL-PURPOSE TRACTORS

The word tractor means "a machine for pulling and pushing." But by connecting different attachments to the front and back, a tractor performs an enormous range of tasks. The heavy engine and hydraulic systems are low down to make the tractor stable, and a strong cab protects the driver if the tractor does roll.

Testing the finished model

Strong cab

Large wheels for extra grip

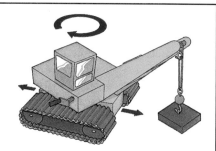

HEAVY LIFTING

The hydraulic system of the tractor can power an arm with a boom, dipper, and bucket. For very heavy loads, a counterweight can be attached at the front.

MODEL CRANE
PART 8

THE FINISHED CRANE

1 TO FINISH YOUR CRANE
Paint all parts of the crane. Then feed a rubber band through the holes in the middle of **F** and **T**. Finally, put a matchstick through the loops at each end to hold **F** and **T** together.

2 WORK THE MODEL
Your model is now complete. You can use it as a crane or add the digger attachment with the bucket.

PULLING

Tractors that are used for plowing the soil need to be able to pull with enormous force. The large back wheels provide good grip and spread the load on soft ground.

Powerful engine

Counterweight

BACKHOE DIGGING

When used with a digging or lifting arm at the back (*below*), hydraulic legs help prevent the tractor from tipping as the load is moved to the side.

BACKHOE DRILL

A shovel can be used as a lever to apply force. By holding the shovel down at the front, the force on the drill increases because the shovel acts as the fulcrum of a lever (*left*).

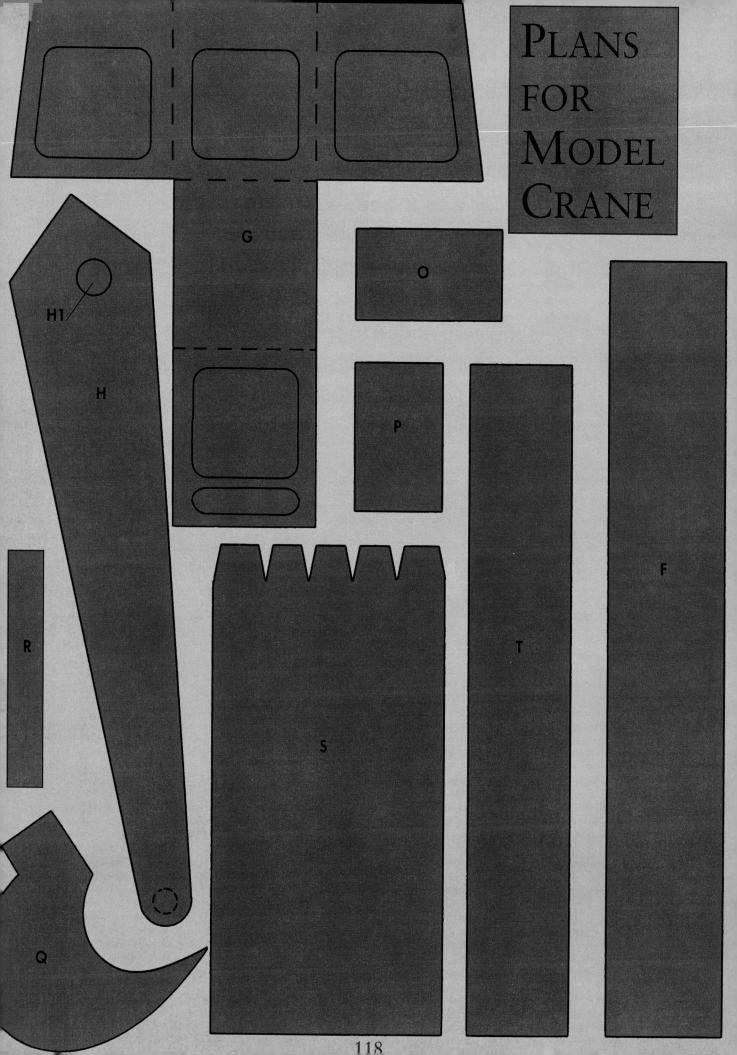

PLANS
FOR
MODEL
CRANE

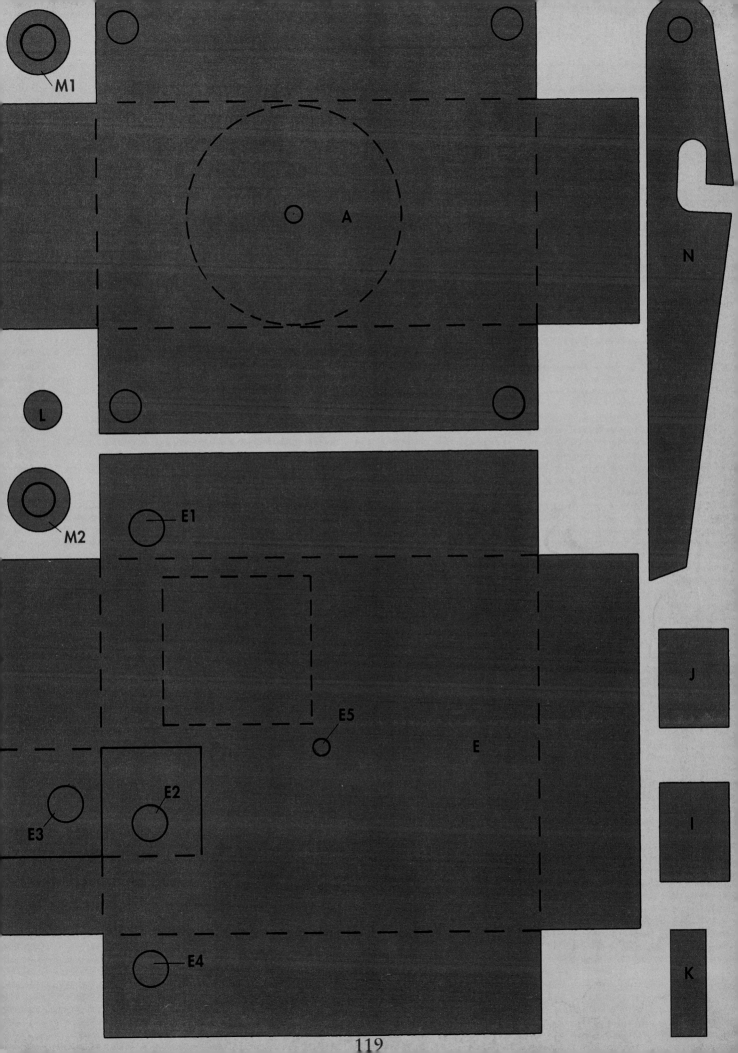

MOTION

SPEED and ACCELERATION

Speed is the distance an object covers in a certain time, and is normally measured in feet per second or miles per hour.

Acceleration is a measure of how quickly an object's speed is changing. The word "acceleration" is normally used for speeding up, but slowing down is also a kind of acceleration (called deceleration).

 (1) How do spacecraft slow down when they reach Earth's atmosphere? All answers are on page 128.

FORCE and POWER

A force is a push or a pull. It has size and direction. Forces can cancel each other out. For example, in a car, thrust pushing forward can be equal to drag pushing backward. In science, power is different from force. It is the rate at which an engine produces energy.

NEWTON'S FIRST LAW

Newton's First Law of Motion states that whenever something moves, even the least bit differently, it is due to a force. When something starts to move, speeds up, slows down, or simply changes direction, there is always a force involved.

(2) Why does a train driver not need to steer a train?

NEWTON'S SECOND LAW

This states that an object's acceleration depends on how big the force moving it is and how heavy the object is. For example, to throw a heavy ball at the same speed as a light one, you need a stronger throw.

NEWTON'S THIRD LAW

When you throw a ball, an equal force pushes back against you. If you were on skates, this force would push you backward (*right*). Newton's Third Law states that whenever anything moves, there is always this balance of forces working in opposite reactions.

MOMENTUM

Everything that is standing still has inertia. This means it won't move unless a force pushes or pulls it. Everything that is moving has momentum. This means it won't slow down or speed up unless something forces it to. Something heavy and fast, like a car, has a lot of momentum. It's the car's momentum that crushes it if it crashes into a wall (*below*).

DRAG and FRICTION

Drag and friction are both forces. Drag is a force that acts on an object, when the object is moving through a liquid or a gas, in the opposite direction to the movement.

Friction is a force between two surfaces in contact with each other that tries to stop the surfaces from rubbing. The greater the force pressing the surfaces together the greater the friction.

Friction occurs when two surfaces are in contact with each other.

? *(3) Can you remember how a ball bearing reduces friction?*

THRUST

Thrust is the name for the force that drives a vehicle forward. It must be strong enough to overcome drag and friction. In boats and planes, propellers or jets create thrust by pushing water or air backward.

GRAVITY

Gravity is the natural force that pulls everything together. Every bit of matter in the universe has its own gravitational pull.

The strength of the pull depends how far apart things are and how big they are —or rather, their mass, which is how much matter they are made of. Big, heavy objects pull harder than small, light objects. This is why Earth's gravity is strong enough to pull us down to the ground, yet we can't even feel an egg's gravity.

? *(4) Why don't rockets have wings? Turn to pages 8-9 if you need help.*

LIFT

Planes overcome the force of gravity by creating lift. Air flowing over their wings creates an upward force greater than the force of gravity, so the plane lifts off the ground. The larger and heavier the plane, the greater the lift must be.

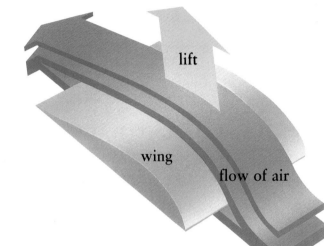

lift

wing

flow of air

BERNOULLI'S PRINCIPLE

Bernoulli's principle (named after an 18th-century scientist) explains how sails work. Sails catch the wind and bow outward into a curved shape. A flat sail works, but not as well. This is because air flowing in front of a curved sail travels faster than the air behind it. This creates lower pressure in front of the sail. The higher pressure behind pushes the sail (and the boat) forward (*below*).

Faster air flow creates low pressure.

Slower air flow creates higher pressure.

ENERGY

WORK and ENERGY

Work is the result of a force moving an object. Energy is the ability of something to do work, or a measure of work done.

HEAT ENERGY

Most energy can be turned easily into a different type of energy. Combustion, or burning, is when the chemical energy in a fuel is turned into heat energy. Heat is also often "waste energy." Have you ever noticed how hot light bulbs get? This is because most of the energy from a candle or a light bulb turns to heat not light.

KINETIC and POTENTIAL ENERGY

Energy comes in two main forms. Potential energy (PE) is stored energy. Kinetic energy (KE) is the energy an object has because it is moving. On a swing, you are constantly changing between having KE and PE.

At the bottom of the swing, you are moving fastest, so your KE is at its greatest. By the time you swing up on the other side, your KE is zero, but your PE is at a maximum because of gravity. If it weren't for drag and friction, you'd swing forever.

KE = 0   KE = 0
PE = Maximum   PE = Maximum

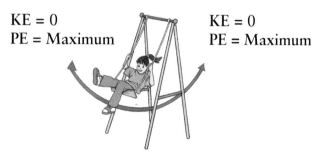

KE = Maximum   PE = Minimum

MACHINES

SIMPLE MACHINES

A machine is a device that does work. All modern machines, however complex, are based in some way on these simple machines used in the ancient world: the wheel, the lever, the pulley, and the ramp.

? *(5) Can you remember what class of lever a wheelbarrow and a seesaw are?*

LEVERS

A lever converts a small force moving a large distance into a big force that moves a short distance. The simplest lever is a rigid bar that twists about a point called the fulcrum. This is a first-class lever (e.g. scales), with the fulcrum between the load and the effort. A second-class lever (e.g. a bottle opener) has the load between the fulcrum and the effort. In a third-class lever (e.g. tweezers), the effort is between the fulcrum and the load.

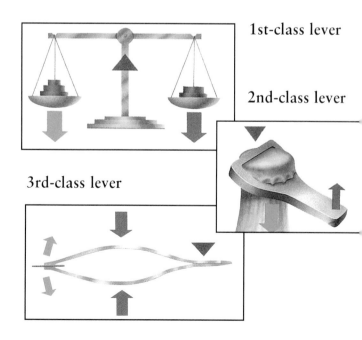

1st-class lever

2nd-class lever

3rd-class lever

WHEELS and AXLES

An axle works like a lever. When it makes a small turn with a big force, the wheel turns a larger distance with a smaller force (*below*). The axle has a smaller circumference, so there is also less friction where it is connected to the vehicle.

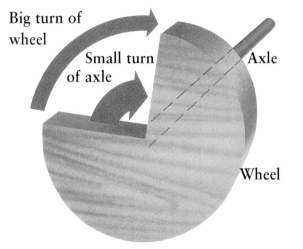

Big turn of wheel

Small turn of axle

Axle

Wheel

PULLEYS

A pulley allows a person to lift something up while staying put on the ground. Several pulleys joined together make a compound pulley (*right*). On a compound pulley, pulling the rope a long way raises a heavy weight a short distance.

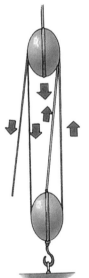

RAMPS

A ramp helps a person increase the distance over which he or she moves an object against the force of gravity. The longer the ramp, the smaller the force needed to lift the load.

SOLIDS and LIQUIDS
SOLID STRUCTURES

Vehicles are made from solid materials such as steel and aluminum. These materials react to stress and strain in different ways. The shape of the vehicle is also very important. For example, a flat piece of cardboard bends easily under a small force. But curved into a cylinder, or bent into an M-shape (*above*), it is much stronger. This is because the force has to compress the cardboard, not simply bend it.

? *(6) Which shape is the strongest—a circle, a square, or a triangle? To find out, try making them from cardboard.*

ELASTICITY

Most solids are elastic, if only a little bit. This means they will return to the same shape again after they have been bent or pulled by a force.

Metals can be made more elastic by bending them into a spring.

Spring at rest

Compressed spring

? *(7) Why do the springs on cars, trucks, and motorcycles work better with shock absorbers?*

WATER PRESSURE

Gravity pulls water toward the center of the Earth. The deeper you go in a body of water, the more water there is above pressing down. If you have ever swum to the bottom of a swimming pool, you may have felt this pressure in your ears. At the bottom of the ocean, this pressure is enormous.

DENSITY

Have you ever noticed it is easier to float in the sea? This is because sea water contains salt and is slightly denser than fresh water. So anything floating in it does not have to sink so far to displace its own weight. You can test this by adding a blob of modeling clay to the end of a straw. The straw floats higher in salty water.

> **?** *(8) Why does a submarine need a very strong hull? Turn to pages 60-61 if you need help.*

DISPLACEMENT

Liquids press sideways and upward. When anything is placed in a liquid, it forces the liquid to move out of the way—a process called displacement. The Greek mathematician Archimedes found that the upward force of the water, the upthrust, is equal to the weight of water displaced.

Upthrust (U) = weight of water displaced (D)

GLOSSARY

Airfoil – the shape a wing needs to be to make air flowing over it create lift.
Altitude – height above the ground.
Balanced – a vehicle or object that does not fall over on its own.
Ballast – the heavy material used to steady a ship that is not carrying cargo.
Bilges – the bottom of a boat where the curved sides meet.
Booster – an additional rocket designed to propel a spacecraft farther on its journey.

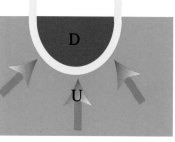

Centrifugal force – a force that seems to throw you outward when you move in a circle. When a satellite is in orbit, this force is exactly balanced by gravity.
Chassis – the supporting framework for the body, engine, and suspension in older cars.
Compound – a system with more than one part, e.g. a compound lever combines two or more levers.
Compressor – a machine that squashes air into a smaller space, creating the high-pressure air that is used in pneumatic systems.
Counterweight – the weight used to balance the load on a crane or truck.
Drag – the resistance of water or air to the movement of an object through it.
Expansion – an increase in size of a gas, liquid, or solid, usually due to heat.
Fiberglass – a light, strong material made by bonding fine glass fibers with a resin (glue).

Fluid – any substance that flows easily, including all gases and liquids.

Fulcrum – the pivot of a lever.

Generator – a device that creates electricity when its central core is spun around. It turns kinetic energy into electrical energy.

Gravity – the force that pulls everything around us down toward the ground. Gravity also pulls any two objects toward each other.

Hydraulic – a machine that uses oil pumped at high pressure to push against a piston.

Jib – the long arm on a crane.

Liquid fuel – rocket fuel carried in liquid form, such as kerosene.

Lubricant – any substance that reduces the friction between two surfaces, such as oil or grease.

Manned Maneuvering Unit – the rocket-powered backpack that moves an astronaut around on spacewalks.

Navigation – plotting the route of a ship, car, or plane.

Orbit – a complete circuit around something—often by a satellite or spacecraft held close to a planet by gravity.

Oxidizer – the source of oxygen needed for liquid fuel to burn.

Payload – the items that are carried on spacecraft, such as astronauts and equipment.

Pitch – the angle of a propeller or rotor.

Pneumatic – a machine that works using compressed (squashed) air.

Recharging – putting electricity into a battery so that the battery can be used again after it has run down.

Satellite – anything that circles another object in space. Moons are natural satellites. Artificial satellites are spacecraft that circle Earth.

Stable – not easy to tip over or upset.

Streamlined – with a smooth shape to reduce drag by allowing air to flow easily over it.

Supersonic – traveling faster than the speed of sound (about 660 mph at 36,000 feet).

Thrust – the "strength" of an engine—that is, how powerfully it pushes.

Traction – the scientific word for grip.

Transmission – a system of shafts and gearboxes that transmits power from the engine to the axles.

Turbulence – random air currents that disturb the air flowing over a wing.

Turbine – a series of blades attached to a shaft. These are turned by hot gas or water flowing over them. They are used in nuclear power plants and all forms of jet engine.

Watertight – an object (such as a boat) that does not let water in (e.g. through cracks or holes).

Welding – sticking two pieces of metal together using molten (melted) metal.

INDEX

INDEX

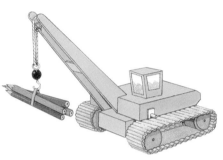

INDEX

? Answers to questions on pages 120-124.

1 A spacecraft relies on friction with the air to slow it down on reentering Earth's atmosphere.

2 The force to make a train go around a curve comes from the track pushing sideways on the wheels.

3 Ball bearings reduce friction because only a small part of them touches the axle they are rubbing against.

4 There is no air in space so wings would be useless. Rockets must use the thrust of their engines instead to counteract gravity.

5 A wheelbarrow is a second-class lever. A seesaw is a first-class lever.

6 The triangular shape is strongest because forces acting on it have to squash the cardboard, as well as bend it.

7 Without shock absorbers, a vehicle would keep bouncing after going over a bump. A shock absorber stops a spring from bouncing back quickly.

8 A submarine needs a very strong hull to protect it from the crushing force of water at great depths. Research submarines have the strongest hulls to withstand the huge pressures at the bottom of the ocean.

PHOTO CREDITS

Abbreviations—t – top, m – middle, b – bottom, r – right, l – left, c – center:
15m—Lockheed Martin. 6t, 15b, 19, 22m, 23b, 29b, 49, 53, 63t, 66, 69, 92, 99—Frank Spooner Pictures. 8, 9 both, 12, 14, 15t, 17, 21, 22b, 23t, 24 all, 25—National Aeronautics and Space Administration (NASA). 37 both, 43, 46-47, 58, 73, 114—Solution Pictures. 28, 42b, 46—Mercedes Benz. 29t, 48—BMW. 42t—Volkswagen. 63m, 70—Pipe Pictures. 76—Lufthansa, Bildarchiv. 77—Pan Am. 79, 89—British Aerospace. 93m—Airbus Industrie. 93mr—Civil Aviation Authority. 100-101—Scania. 104—JCB. 96-97, 98—CAT. 97bl, 113, 116, 117l, 117tr—Renault. 97tr, 100bl—Liebherr. 100c, 117mr, 117bl—John Deere. 103, 109br—Select Pictures. 106t—Sunderland Shipbuilders. 109tl—Digital Stock. 112—Paul Nightingale.

1736